Teach® Yourself

Get started in Swedish

Ivo Holmqvist
Ingwor Holmqvist
Vera Croghan

First published in Great Britain in 2013 by Hodder & Stoughton. An Hachette UK company.

This edition published 2013

British Library Cataloguing in Publication Data: a catalogue record for this title is available from the British Library.

Library of Congress Catalog Card Number: on file.

ISBN 9781444175202

3

Typeset by Cenveo® Publisher Services.

Advisory editor: Beth Beemer

Printed and bound in Great Britain by Clays Ltd, Elcograf S.p.A.

Hodder & Stoughton policy is to use papers that are natural, renewable and recyclable products and made from wood grown in sustainable forests. The logging and manufacturing processes are expected to conform to the environmental regulations of the country of origin.

Hodder & Stoughton Ltd
Carmelite House
50 Victoria Embankment London
EC4Y 0DZ

www.hodder.co.uk

The authorized representative in the EEA is Hachette Ireland, 8 Castlecourt Centre, Dublin 15, D15 XTP3, Ireland (email: info@hbgi.ie)

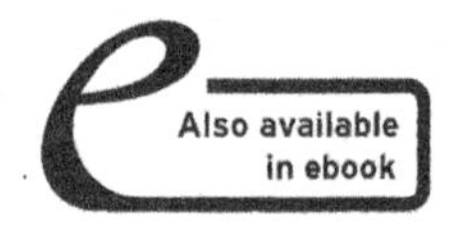

Contents

About the authors

Having met at Lund University while studying Scandinavian Languages, English, Comparative Literature, Art History, Ethnology and History of Religion, we headed for New Zealand for our first academic jobs, managing the Scandinavian Department at Auckland University. Then we took posts teaching Swedish language and literature at the universities of Odense and Århus in Denmark, and Swedish, English and Art History at Grännaskolan, an international boarding school in southern Sweden. Back in Auckland, we ran Scandinavian Studies once more until the department closed down in 2001. After a brief sojourn at Europaskolan, another international high school, this time near Stockholm, Ingwor taught at Katedralskolan and at the pharmaceutical company Astra Zeneca, both in Lund, and Ivo took up the chair in Scandinavian Literature at the University of Ghent in Belgium. Since 2008, we have again been living in New Zealand, running the Scandinavian Light bed and breakfast in West Auckland. Ivo has written a number of books, two of them on the Danish authors Hans Christian Andersen and Karen Blixen/Isak Dinesen, and his PhD thesis centred on the Anglo-Welsh writer Richard Hughes.

Ingwor and Ivo Holmqvist

I was born in Sweden and took my MA (filosofie magister) degree in Scandinavian Languages, English and Comparative Literature at Lund University. While studying, I also worked in the office of Folkuniversitetet, which organizes lectures and courses led by university teachers or students who have passed their exams in the relevant subjects. One of my duties was to occasionally stand in for teachers. Thus I got to teach Swedish to foreign students who had to learn Swedish before commencing their university courses. I enjoyed teaching these courses, which also helped me to get my first full-time job teaching Swedish at Aberdeen University. I moved to Norwich when the University of East Anglia opened and have taught Swedish there for well over 30 years. My textbook *Teach Yourself Complete Swedish* was first published in 1995, with many subsequent editions, the later ones written in co-operation with Ivo Holmqvist.

Vera Croghan

How this book works

Swedish is a Scandinavian language closely related to Norwegian and Danish – Swedes, Danes and Norwegians have few or no problems understanding each other – and more distantly to Icelandic and Faroese. It is spoken by a good 10 million Swedes (and as a second language by 1 million immigrants to Sweden). It is one of the two official languages in Finland, spoken by 5.5 per cent of the population, and spoken and understood also by many in the Finnish-speaking majority (Finnish is a Finno-Ugrian language, unrelated to the Scandinavian ones). Swedish is the native tongue of some 300,000 expatriate Swedes, and ranks as the 50th most common language in the United States.

Swedish and English are fairly closely related, and you will find many instantly recognizable words in this book. In the Indo-European group of languages, Swedish is a North Germanic one as are the other Scandinavian languages; English a West Germanic one as are German and Dutch. Thus speakers of English, German and Dutch will find learning Swedish comparatively easy (Scandinavians will have no problem at all). Pronunciation will have very few hurdles, as explained later in this book.

- **What you will learn** identifies what you should be able to do in Swedish by the end of the unit.
- **Culture points** present cultural aspects related to the themes in the units, introducing key words and phrases and including follow-up questions.
- **Vocabulary builder** introduces key unit vocabulary grouped by theme and conversation, accompanied by audio. By learning the words and listening to them, your progress in learning contemporary Swedish will be swift.
- **Conversations** are recorded dialogues that you can listen to and practise, beginning with a narrative that helps you understand what you are going to hear, with a focusing question and follow-up activities.
- **Language discovery** draws your attention to key language points in the conversations and to rules of grammar and pronunciation. Read the notes and look at the conversations to see how the language is used in practice.
- **Practice** offers a variety of exercises, including speaking opportunities, to give you a chance to see and use words and phrases in their context.

- **Speaking and listening** offer practice in speaking and understanding Swedish through exercises that let you use what you have learned in previous units.
- **Reading and writing** provide practice in reading everyday items and contain mostly vocabulary from the unit. Try to get the main point of the text before you answer the follow-up questions.
- **Test yourself** helps you assess what you have learned. You learn more by doing the tests without consulting the text, and only when you have done them check if your answers are the correct ones (do not cheat!).
- **Self-check** lets you see what you can do after having completed each unit.

To help you through the course, a system of icons indicates the actions to take:

Listen to audio

Speak Swedish out loud

Figure something out

Culture tip

Exercises coming up

Reading passage

Write and make notes

Check your progress

Here are some further resources in the book for you to consult:

- **Useful expressions** lists commonly used everyday phrases.
- **Review units** sum up what you have learned in the previous units. There are three reviews: after Unit 3, after Unit 6 and after Unit 10. If you master all questions in the review unit, go ahead, if not, go back and refresh your knowledge.
- The **Answer key** helps you check your progress by including answers to the activities both in the text units and the review units.

Once you have done all ten units in this book successfully, you may want to proceed with more advanced Swedish textbooks, such as *Teach Yourself Complete Swedish* which follows much the same outline as *Get started in Swedish*. Bilingual dictionaries and Swedish grammars will be of much use, and there are also internet resources for learning Swedish.

Learn to learn

The Discovery method

This book incorporates the Discovery method of learning. You will be encouraged throughout the course to engage your mind and figure out the meaning for yourself, through identifying patterns and understanding grammatical concepts, noticing words that are similar to English, and more. As a result of your efforts, you will be able to retain what you have learned, use it with confidence and continue to learn the language on your own after you have finished this book.

Everyone can succeed in learning a language – the key is to know how to learn it. Learning is more than just reading or memorizing grammar and vocabulary. It is about being an active learner, learning in real contexts and using in different situations what you have learned. If you figure something out for yourself, you are more likely to understand it, and when you use what you have learned, you are more likely to remember it.

As many of the essential details, such as grammar rules, are introduced through the Discovery method, you will have more fun while learning. The language will soon start to make sense and you will be relying on your own intuition to construct original sentences independently, not just by listening and repeating.

Happy learning!

Pronunciation guide

Speaking Swedish is easy once you know the basic pronunciation rules. Listen to the soundtracks in this book, look at Swedish films (seldom dubbed), listen on the net to Swedish radio programmes (www.sr.se) and follow the Swedish TV News *Aktuellt* and *Rapport* (www.svt.se). When you visit Sweden, take every opportunity to speak Swedish even if the Swedes themselves will grab every chance to practise their English skills on a native speaker of that language. There are many excellent ways for you to get going in Swedish and to keep refining your command of both its spoken and written varieties.

The most important thing to remember when pronouncing Swedish words is that all letters should be pronounced distinctly, even unstressed end vowels, and vowels and consonants in endings, e.g. **pojke** (*boy*), **före** (*before*), **medan** (*while*), **trädet** (*the tree*).

The Swedish alphabet has 29 letters. Their names (in brackets) are used when spelling words out loud.

00.01

A a	(a)	**K k**	(kå)	**U u**	(u)
B b	(be)	**L l**	(ell)	**V v**	(ve)
C c	(se)	**M m**	(em)	**W w**	(dubbel ve)
D d	(de)	**N n**	(en)	**X x**	(eks)
E e	(e)	**O o**	(o)	**Y y**	(y)
F f	(eff)	**P p**	(pe)	**Z z**	(säta)
G g	(ge)	**Q q**	(ku)	**Å å**	(å)
H h	(hå)	**R r**	(ärr)	**Ä ä**	(ä)
I i	(i)	**S s**	(ess)	**Ö ö**	(ö)
J j	(ji)	**T t**	(te)		

The last three letters are vowels; this means that Swedish has nine vowels, as **y** is always a vowel in Swedish. The vowels are **a**, **e**, **i**, **o**, **u**, **y**, **å**, **ä**, **ö**.

The vowels in Swedish are pure sounds, not a combination of two sounds (diphthongs) as they often are in English. Diphthongs only occur in dialects.

Vowels

Swedish vowels may be long or short, but vowel length is connected with stress. A stressed vowel is more prominent than the other letters in the word.

00.01

A stressed vowel is long:

- as end-vowel in words of one syllable: **ja**, **vi**, **nu**, **se**, **två**.
- before a single consonant in the same syllable (for exceptions see below): **mor**, **far**, **vara**, **heta**, **gata**, **jul**.

A stressed vowel is short:

- before two or more consonants in the same syllable: **flicka**, **gubbe** (*old man*), **äpple**, **kall**, **kopp** (except before **-r**: **barn**, **lärd** (*learned*)).
- in a few common words of one syllable: **han**, **hon**, **den**, **min**, **din**, **sin**.
- often in words of one syllable ending in **-m** or **-n**: **vem**, **hem**, **kom**, **kam**, **som**, **rum**, **dum**, **man**, **in**, **kan**, **men**, **mun**, **än**.

An unstressed vowel is always short: the last **a** in **tala**, **resa**; the **e** in **pojken**, **åker**, etc.

The vowels are divided into two groups:

a, **o**, **u**, **å** are hard vowels

e, **i**, **y**, **ä**, **ö** are soft vowels.

This distinction is important in explaining the different pronunciations of the consonants **g** and **k**, and the consonant combination **sk** before the different vowel groups.

00.01

Swedish letter	Pronunciation	Example
long **a**	like *a* in *father*	**far** (*father*)
short **a**	like the *u* sound in *but*	**katt** (*cat*)
long **e**	no English equivalent. A little like *e* in *ear*, but with the tongue muscles very tense	**med** (*with*)
short **e**	like *e* in *men*	**penna** (*pen*)
long **i**	like *ea* in *heat*	**liv** (*life*)
short **i**	like *i* in *kiss*	**hiss** (*lift*)
long **o**	like *oo* in *moon* with tightly rounded lips	**bok** (*book*)

short **o**	like *oo* in *book* with less tightly rounded lips	**blomma** (*flower*)
long **u**	no English equivalent. Start with the *u*- sound in *true*, but round the lips very tightly	**hus** (*house*)
short **u**	like *u* in *full*, but not so tensely rounded lips as the long *u*	**hund** (*dog*)
long **y**	no English equivalent. Like the long **i** but with tightly rounded lips	**ny** (*new*)
short **y**	no English equivalent. Sounds like the short **i** but with rounded lips	**syster** (*sister*)
long **å**	like the *aw* sound in *raw*	**gå** (*go*)
short **å**	like *o* in *Scot*	**åtta** (*eight*)
long **ä**	like the first vowel in the diphthong *ea* in *bear*	**äta** (*eat*)
short **ä**	more open than the English *e* in *set*	**lätt** (*easy*)
long **ö**	no equivalent in English. The tongue is in the same position as for *e* but the lips are rounded and protruded	**söt** (*sweet*)
short **ö**	like the *u*- sound in *curt* but shorter	**böcker** (*books*)

In the short vowels the mouth is often slightly more open than in the long vowels. This is most noticeable when an **ä** or **ö** is followed by an **r**, for example:

Long vowels	Short vowels
här (*here*)	**härja** (*ravage*)
lära (*teach*)	**lärde** (*taught*)
hör (*hears*)	**hörde** (*heard*)
dör (*dies*)	**dörr** (*door*)

Consonants

 00.01

Swedish letter	Pronunciation	Example
b	like *b* in *bad*	**bo** (*live*)
c	found mainly in words of foreign origin. As a rule, it represents the same sound as in the foreign word. Thus it is pronounced as *s* in front of the soft vowels (**e**, **i**, **y**, **ä**, **ö**) but as *k* in front of the hard vowels (**a**, **o**, **u**, **å**) in stressed syllables, and always as *k* in front of **k**	**cykel** (bicycle), **cancer** (*cancer*), **flicka** (*girl*)
d	approximately as in English, but with the tongue just behind the upper teeth	**dam** (*lady*)
f	like *f* in *firm*	**fem** (*five*)
g	like *g* in *go* in front of the hard vowels (**a**, **o**, **u**, **å**) or consonants in stressed syllables like *j* in front of the soft vowels (**e**, **i**, **y**, **ä**, **ö**) in stressed syllables like *j* finally after **l** and **r**	**gata** (*street*), **god** (*good*), **Gud** (*God*), **gå** (*go*), **gris** (*pig*), **ge** (*give*), **gissa** (*guess*), **gyllene** (*golden*), **gäss** (*geese*), **göra** (*do, make*), **älg** (*elk*), **berg** (*mountain*)
h	like *h* in *hot*	**het** (*hot*)
j	like *y* in *you*	**ja** (*yes*)
k	like *k* in *keep* in front of the hard vowels (**a**, **o**, **u**, **å**) or consonants in stressed syllables	**kan** (*can*), **ko** (*cow*), **kunde** (*could*), **kål** (*cabbage*), **klo** (*claw*)

k	like *ch* in *church* in front of the soft vowels (**e**, **i**, **y**, **ä**, **ö**) in stressed syllables	**kedja** (*chain*), **kind** (*cheek*), **kyss** (*kiss*), **kära** (*dear*), **köpa** (*buy*)
l	like *l* in *leaf*	**liv** (*life*)
m	like *m* in *me*	**mor** (*mother*)
n	like *n* in *no*	**ny** (*new*)
p	like *p* in *plate*	**plats** (*place*)
q	like *k* in *king*	**quiche** (*quiche*)
r	a rolled *r* made with the tip of the tongue in central and northern Sweden; in the south it is not rolled but made with the root of the tongue at the back of the mouth	**ren** (*clean*)
s	like voiceless *s* in *see*. In Swedish **s** is never voiced as in *measure*	**se** (*see*)
t	pronounced with the tongue just behind the upper teeth	**tand** (*tooth*)
v	like *v* in *very*	**vem** (*who*)
w	like *v* in *very*. It only occurs in names and words of foreign origin	**WC** (*toilet*)
x	like *ks*, never like *gz* as in *example*	**herr X** (*Mr X*)
z	like voiceless *s* in *see*. It only occurs in names and words of foreign origin	**zoo** (*zoo*)
ng	like *ng* in *ring*, never like *ngg* as in *England*	**ung** (*young*)
gn	like *ngn*	**regn** (*rain*)
sk	like *sk* in *skate* in front of the hard vowels (**a**, **o**, **u**, **å**) or consonants in stressed syllables	**ska** (*shall*), **sko** (*shoe*), **skulle** (*should*), **skål** (*cheers*), **skriva** (*write*)

	like *sh* in *she* in front of the soft vowels (**e**, **i**, **y**, **ä**, **ö**) in stressed syllables	**sked** (*spoon*), **skina** (*shine*), **skygg** (*shy*), **skär** (*pink*), **skön** (*comfortable*)
sch, sj, skj	like *sh* in *she*	**marsch** (*march*), **sjö** (*lake*), **skjuta** (*shoot*),
stj, si(on), ti(on)	like *sh* in *she*	**stjärna** (*star*), **passion** (*passion*), **station** (*station*)
kj, tj	like *ch* in *Charles* without the initial *t*- sound	**kjol** (*skirt*), **tjock** (*thick*)

00.01

Note: **d**, **g**, **h**, **l** are mute in front of **j** at the beginning of words or in compound words when these consonants belong to the same syllable: **djup** (*deep*), **gjort** (*done, made*), **hjul** (*wheel*), **ljud** (*sound*).

k followed by **n** is pronounced (unlike in English): **kniv** (*knife*), **knä** (*knee*). Swedes use **ck** instead of **kk**: **flicka** (*girl*), **mycket** (*very*).

q, **w**, **x**, **z** only occur in names and foreign words. Then **q** is pronounced like a *k*, and **w** is pronounced like a *v*. **Qu** is pronounced like *kv*, e.g. **Qatar**, **WC** (*toilet*), **Wennergren**, **Quist**, **Quinnan** (in old texts or jokingly = *woman*). **X** is pronounced like *ks*, e.g. **extra** (*extra*), and **z** is pronounced like voiceless *s*, e.g. **zebra** (*zebra*).

00.01

t is pronounced in **nation** (*nation*) and **motion** (*exercise*).

l is mute in **karl** (*man*) and **värld** (*world*).

rs is pronounced like *sh* in *mash* in central and northern Sweden, but not in the south, where the two letters are pronounced individually, e.g. **person** (*person*).

In **rd**, **rl, rt, rn** the **r** is assimilated with the following consonant so that these are pronounced almost like their English equivalents in central and northern Sweden. In the south of Sweden the two letters are pronounced individually, e.g. **hård** (*hard*), **svårt** (*difficult*), **härlig** (*glorious*), **barn** (*child*).

Stress

Swedish has *sentence stress* (the words that are most significant for the meaning are stressed) and *word stress* (different syllables in words are stressed).

00.01

Word stress. The stress is normally on the first syllable of every word except in a number of loan words from other languages where there is no completely reliable rule. A great many now follow Swedish pronunciation rules, at least in part, but others may retain the stress on the syllable that carried the stress in the original language. That is usually the case with words of French or Latin origin, e.g. **restaurang** (*restaurant*), **novell** (*short story*), **museum** (*museum*), **studera** (*study*).

If a word begins with the prefixes **be-**, **för-**, **ge-**, the stress is on the syllable following these prefixes, e.g. **betala** (*pay*), **förstå** (*understand*), **gedigen** (*solid*).

Accent

Swedish is a tone language, which means that more than one tone may be used in one word. That is why it sounds as if Swedes are singing when they speak. There are two such word accents in Swedish: 'single tone' (also called *accent 1* or *acute accent*) and 'double tone' (also called *accent 2* or *grave accent*).

00.01

Single tone, as in English, is used in words of one syllable. Note that even when a one-syllable word takes an ending, it keeps its single tone accent, e.g. **boll** (*ball*) – **bollen** (*the ball*), **hund** (*dog*) – **hunden** (*the dog*).

Single tone is also used in many two-syllable words ending in **-el**, **-en**, **-er**, e.g. **cykel** (*bicycle*), **vatten** (*water*), **vinter** (*winter*), and in present tense verb forms ending in **-er**, e.g. **reser** (*travel*).

00.01

Double tone is used in most words of more than one syllable and in most compound nouns, e.g. **flicka** (*girl*), **trädgård** (*garden*), as well as in verb forms ending in **-a**, **-ar**, **-ade**, **-at**, **-ad**, e.g. **tala**, **talar**, **talade**, **talat**, **talad** (*speak, spoke, spoken*). In words with double tone the main stress is on the first syllable – a falling tone, but there is also a strong secondary stress on the second syllable – a rising tone, e.g. **lampan** (*the lamp*), **spela** (*play*).

Single tone	Double tone
boll	flicka
bollen	trädgård
cykel	tala
reser	lampa

The difference in tone is used to distinguish between words which are spelt the same way but mean different things, for example:

Single tone	Double tone
anden (*the duck*)	**anden** (*the spirit*)
biten (*the bit*)	**biten** (*bitten*)

Note: The line indicates the pitch, i.e. the height of the tone of your voice.

Everyday pronunciation

00.01

The written language and the spoken language do differ. Note the following forms of words commonly used in normal speech:

- The final consonant is normally dropped in some very common words: **ja/g** (*I*), **da/g** (*day*), **va/d** (*what*), **go/d** (*good*), **me/d** (*with*), **de/t** (*it*), **mycke/t** (*much*).
- **Och** (*and*) is usually pronounced as **å**, and **nej** (*no*) is pronounced as **nä**.
- In normal speech some words are pronounced differently from how they are written: **mig** (*me, myself*), **dig** (*you, yourself*), **sig** (*himself, herself, itself, themselves*) are pronounced as **mej**, **dej**, **sej**, and they are sometimes written this way as well. **De** (*they*) and **dem** (*them*) are pronounced as **dåmm** and sometimes written **dom** in colloquial contexts. **Någon**, **något**, **några** (*somebody/anybody, something/anything, some/any*) are pronounced **nån**, **nåt**, **nåra**. **Sådan** (*such*) is pronounced **sån**. **Sedan** (*afterwards*) is pronounced **sen**. **Mera** and **mer** (*more*, for uncountables) and **flera** and **fler** (*more*, for countables) are used interchangeably.
- Adjectives ending in **-ig** usually drop the **-g** in the spoken language, for example: **roli/g** (*funny*), **tråki/g** (*boring*).

- The past tense of the verbs **säga** (*say*) and **lägga** (*lay*) are written **sade** and **lade** but pronounced **sa** and **la**. **Skall** (*shall*) is pronounced **ska** and now normally also written this way.
- The imperatives **tag** (*take*) and **drag** (*pull*) are pronounced **ta** and **dra**, and nowadays often written this way too.
- The present tense **är** (*is*) is pronounced **e**.

Hej! God dag!

Hello! Goodbye!

In this unit, you will learn how to:

- ***say hello and goodbye.***
- ***introduce yourself and others.***
- ***say where you come from and where you live.***
- ***use personal pronouns.***
- ***use the present tense of verbs.***
- ***ask questions.***

CEFR: (A1) *Can introduce yourself and others and can ask and answer questions about personal details such as where someone lives.*

Greetings

Hej is the most common phrase when meeting someone, often repeated as **hej hej**, while **hej då** is used when saying goodbye. Slightly more formal are **god dag** and **adjö** for *hello* and *goodbye*. Depending on the time of the day, **hej** and **god dag** can be replaced by **god morgon**, **god middag**, **god kväll** and **god natt**.

What do you think these greetings used at different times of the day mean? **God morgon**, **God middag**, **God kväll**, **God natt**

SPEAKING DIFFERENT LANGUAGES

En svensk i Sverige talar svenska, en engelsman i England och en amerikan i USA talar engelska. A Swede in Sweden speaks Swedish, a Briton in England and an American in the United States speak English.

In Swedish, the word for most languages carries the **-ska** ending: for the Nordic region **svenska**, **norska**, **danska**, **isländska** and **finska**. These are the corresponding countries: **Sverige**, **Norge**, **Danmark**, **Island** and **Finland**.

I Frankrike (*France*) **talar man franska, i Tyskland** (*Germany*) **tyska, i Ryssland** (*Russia*) **ryska, i Italien** (*Italy*) **italienska och i Spanien** (*Spain*) **spanska.**

Vocabulary builder

01.01 **Look at the words and phrases and complete the missing English expressions. Then listen and try to imitate the pronunciation of the speakers.**

GREETINGS

Tjenare! Tjena!	*Hello!* (both are very informal)
Hejsan!	______
Läget?/Hur är läget?	*How are things?* (less formal)
Hur är det? Hur står det till?	______
Hur mår du?	*How are you feeling?*
Jag mår bra/utmärkt	*I'm doing well*

SAYING GOODBYE

Hej då!	*Goodbye!* (less formal)
Adjö! Ajö!	*Goodbye!* (more formal)

NEW EXPRESSIONS

Look at the words and expressions that are used in the following conversation. Note their meanings.

Vad heter du?	*What is your name?*
Jag heter...	*My name is...*
Var kommer du från?	*Where do you come from?*
Jag kommer från...	*I come from...*
Hon är svenska.	*She is Swedish.*
Han är amerikan.	*He is American.*
flyga	*to fly*
vart	*where*
jobba	*work*
göra	*do*
så intressant	*how interesting*
bo	*live*
gå	*to go, depart*
bra	*good, well*
resa	*to travel*
nästa vecka	*next week*
visitkort	*business card*

Some Swedish nouns are the same in singular and plural:

ett flyg, flera flyg	*one plane, many planes*
ett kort, många kort	*one card, many cards*

Conversation 1

01.02 *Lisbeth Wallander sits at a table in the coffee lounge at Arlanda airport, waiting for her flight to depart. Ben Anderson asks if he can share her table.*

1 How do they greet each other and how do they say goodbye?

Ben	Hej, kan jag sitta här?
Lisbeth	Ja, det går bra.
Ben	Jag flyger till New York. Vart ska du?
Lisbeth	Jag flyger till London.
Ben	Jaha, vad jobbar du med?
Lisbeth	Jag är datakonsult. Vad gör du?
Ben	Jag är journalist.
Lisbeth	Så intressant. Vad heter du?
Ben	Jag heter Ben Anderson och bor i New York. Och vad heter du?
Lisbeth	Jag heter Lisbeth Wallander och jag bor här i Stockholm.
Ben	När går ditt flyg?
Lisbeth	Det går snart.
Ben	Ha en bra resa.
Lisbeth	Tack det samma. Jag är i New York nästa vecka.
Ben	Ring när du kommer. Här har du mitt visitkort.
Lisbeth	Nu måste jag gå till gaten. Då ses vi snart igen. Hej då!

2 Read the conversation again and answer the questions.

a Where is Lisbeth travelling to?
b What does Lisbeth do for a living?
c What does Ben do for a living?
d Where does Lisbeth live?

Language discovery

1 Look at the conversation again. How do you translate the following sentences?

a I am a journalist.

b Where are you flying to?

2 How does Ben say the following? What do you notice about the end of the verb in each case?

a My name is Ben Anderson.

b I live in New York.

3 Ben and Lisbeth ask each other questions. What words do they use for the following?

a What

b Where

1 PERSONAL PRONOUNS

Personal pronouns are used to replace a noun. They are shown in the following table with the corresponding object forms.

jag	*I*	**mig**	*me*
du	*you*	**dig**	*you*
han	*he*	**honom**	*him*
hon	*she*	**henne**	*her*
den (non-neuter), **det** (neuter)	*it*	**den** **det**	*it*
vi	*we*	**oss**	*us*
ni	*you*	**er**	*you*
de (often pronounced **dom**)	*they*	**dem**	*them*

Here are some examples of these in use, with the verb **möter**.

Jag möter dig, du möter mig. *I meet you, you meet me.*

Hon möter honom, han möter henne. *He meets her, she meets him.*

Vi möter er, ni möter oss. *We meet you, you meet us.*

2 VERBS IN THE PRESENT TENSE

Swedish verbs in the present tense end in **-r**.

Jag bor i Stockholm.	*I live in Stockholm.*
Du bor i New York.	*You live in New York.*
Han bor i London.	*He lives in London.*
Vi bor i Sverige.	*We live in Sweden.*
Ni bor i USA.	*You live in the USA.*
De bor i England.	*They live in England.*

Jag är svensk och bor i Stockholm, jobbar på IKEA, kommer hem, läser en bok, mår bra, förstår och talar engelska, och går på bio . I am a Swede living in Stockholm, working at IKEA, I come home, read a book, feel fine, I understand and speak English, and I go to the cinema.

Är (*am, are, is*), **bor** (*live, lives*), **jobbar** (*work, works*), **kommer** (*come, comes*), **läser** (*read, reads*), **mår** (*feel, feels*), **förstår** (*understand, understands*), **talar** (*speak, speaks*), **går** (*go, goes*)

3 ASKING QUESTIONS

The basic question words in Swedish are shown in the following table.

när	*when*
var	*where*
hur	*how*
varför	*why*
vem	*who*
vad	*what*
vilken	*which*

Some question words reveal either position or direction:

Var är du? Varifrån kommer du? Vart går du?

Var? (position) **Varifrån?** (direction) **Vart?** (direction)

The Swedish for *here* and *there* is either **här** or **hit**, **där** or **dit.**

Jag är här, du kommer hit. Han är där, hon reser dit.

Practice

1 Match the Swedish to the English.

a Hon möter honom — **1** I meet you

b Vi möter er — **2** You meet me

c Du möter mig
d Han möter henne
e Ni möter oss
f Vi möter dem
g De möter mig
h Jag möter dig

3 She meets him
4 He meets her
5 We meet you (plural)
6 You (plural) meet us
7 We meet them
8 They meet me

2 Translate the sentences into Swedish.

a I am Swedish.
b You live in New York.
c She meets him in America.
d I feel fine.
e They go to the gate.

3 Match the Swedish to the English.

a Hur mår du?
b Ha en bra dag!
c Vi ses snart igen.
d Jag bor här.
e Tack det samma.

1 Thank you, likewise.
2 I live here.
3 How are you?
4 Have a nice day!
5 See you soon.

Conversation 2

01.03 *Oskar and Filip have not met for a long time when they suddenly run into each other.*

1 What are their jobs?

Oskar Tjena Filip! Hur är läget?
Filip Jodå, skapligt (*not too bad*). Själv då?
Oskar Jo tack, det knallar (*Thanks, I am OK*). Vad gör du nuförtiden (*nowadays*)?
Filip Jag jobbar som fotbollstränare. Vad gör du?
Oskar Jag har ett hyfsat (*quite OK*) jobb som ingenjör.
Filip Låter kul. Bra betalt?
Oskar Tja, lagom för att klara familjen.
Filip Hänger du med på bio på torsdag?
Oskar Gärna, om jag kan ordna barnvakt.
Filip Jag fixar biljetter så ses vi där. Ha det bra till dess.
Oskar Du med. Hej på dej.

2 Read the conversation above and answer the questions.

a Does Oskar like his job?

b Is he well paid?

c Will he come along to the cinema?

d Who is buying the tickets?

3 Now listen to the conversation line by line and repeat out loud.

Speaking

01.04 **Listen to the conversation once more, then play the part of Filip in this conversation.**

Oskar	Tjena Filip! Hur är läget?
Filip	I am fine. And you?
Oskar	Jo tack, det knallar. Vad gör du nuförtiden?
Filip	I work as a football trainer. What do you do?
Oskar	Jag har ett hyfsat jobb som ingenjör.
Filip	That sounds good. Is it well paid?
Oskar	Tja, lagom för att klara familjen.
Filip	Would you like to come along to the cinema next Thursday?
Oskar	Gärna, om jag kan ordna barnvakt.
Filip	I´ll take care of the tickets. See you there. Keep well until then.

Reading

Read this summary of the first conversation, and answer the questions:

Ben och Lisbeth väntar på sina flyg på Arlanda, Stockholms internationella flygplats. De säger sina namn och var de bor. Lisbeth är datakonsult och ska flyga till London. Ben är journalist och ska flyga hem till New York. Lisbeth ska ringa till Ben när hon är i New York nästa vecka.

a What are Ben and Lisbeth doing at the airport?
b Have they met before?
c What will Lisbeth do when she is in New York?

Writing

Rearrange the words into sentences, beginning with the one that starts with a capital letter.

Example: affärsresa på London till Jag ska

Jag ska på affärsresa till London

a dagis hämta på ska barnen Jag
b du med torsdag på på Hänger bio?
c barnvakt jag om ordna Gärna kan

Test yourself

1 Translate the following sentences into Swedish using the present tense.

a She is going to London.

b I am a journalist.

c My name is Lisbeth Wallander and I live in Stockholm.

2 Insert the pronoun indicated in brackets into each sentence.

a Hon möter (her).

b (We) möter henne.

c Ni möter (us).

d (You plural) möter mig.

3 How would you ask the following questions?

a Where do you live?

b What is your name?

c How are you?

4 How would you greet the following people?

a Your friend

b Your boss when getting to work in the morning

c Your family at bedtime

SELF CHECK

I CAN...
... say hello and goodbye.
... introduce myself and others.
... say where I come from and where I live.
... use personal pronouns.
... use the present tense.
... ask questions.

Min familj och andra släktingar

My family and other relatives

In this unit, you will learn how to:

- ***describe your family.***
- ***answer questions.***
- ***talk about the seasons.***
- ***form the plural of nouns.***

CEFR: (A1) *Can recognize familiar words and phrases concerning yourself and your family.* **(A2)** *Can write about everyday aspects of your environment.*

Relatives

The Swedish for *mother* and *father* is **mamma** and **pappa** (plural: **mammor** and **pappor**), or less commonly **mor** and **far** (plural **mödrar** and **fäder**). They are your **föräldrar** (*parents*). In Swedish the words you use for relatives indicate if they are relatives on your mother's side or on your father's. Thus your *uncle* is either your **morbror** or your **farbror**, and your *aunt* either your **moster** or your **faster**. Your *grandparents* are either your **mormor** and **morfar** or your **farmor** and **farfar**. This also applies to great-grandparents and beyond where you just add **mor** or **far** for each generation: **mormorsmor**, **farfarsfar**, etc. You can also tell if your *grandsons* and *granddaughters* (**barnbarn**) are children of your daughter or your son: **dotterson** and **dotterdotter** would be your daughter's children, for example. Their children in turn are your **barnbarnsbarn**. Your **svåger** is the man who married your sister, your **svägerska** the woman who married your brother, and **svärföräldrar** are the parents of your spouse.

If you use **dotterson** and **dotterdotter** for your daughter's children, what words would you use for the children of your son?

Fathers and Sons is a novel by Ivan Turgenev and a short story by Ernest Hemingway. What is the Swedish title?

Vocabulary builder

02.01 **Look at the words and phrases and complete the missing English equivalents. Then listen and imitate the pronunciation of the speakers as closely as possible.**

FAMILY MEMBERS

man	*husband*
fru (or hustru)	*wife*
morföräldrar	______
farföräldrar	______
syster (plural systrar)	*sister (sisters)*
bror (or broder)	*brother*
syskon	*sibling*
kusin	*cousin*

SEASONS

årstid	*season*
vinter	______
vår	*spring*
sommar	______
höst	*autumn*

NEW EXPRESSIONS

Look at the words and expressions that are used in the following conversation. Note their meanings.

kul att ses	*good to see you*
ha det bra	*take care*
eftersom	*because*
tyvärr, dessvärre	*unfortunately*
turas om	*take turns*
barnpassning	*childcare*
förenkla	*simplify*

Dagis is where children are looked after during the day while their parents work, also called **lekskola** (**lekis**). **Förskola** is the general term for daycare for children aged one to six, after which they start school, compulsory for nine years (**grundskola**).

Conversation 1

02.02 *It is a long time since Susanna talked to her friend Lena. Now they happen to meet outside the pre-school.*

1 How has Lena solved daycare for her children?

Susanna	Men hej, Lena, det var länge sedan! Hur mår du?
Lena	Tack, bara bra! Du själv?
Susanna	Jotack, jag har precis varit och lämnat av Pelle på dagis, och sedan hämtar min man honom på hemväg från jobbet.
Lena	Så bra. Mina barn är hos mormor och morfar två dagar i veckan, och hos farmor och farfar de andra dagarna, och det fungerar jättebra.
Susanna	Utmärkt! Vi har ju inte släkt i närheten, tyvärr, mina bröder bor båda i Stockholm, och min mans syster, min svägerska, bor i Malmö, så mina barn har inga kusiner alls här.
Lena	Trist. Ja, vi har tur, med både morföräldrar och farföräldrar nära, och även min syster och hennes familj, så vi kan alltid turas om med barnpassning.
Susanna	Ja, det förenklar ju vardagen, när man har familjen nära. Nu måste jag handla middagsmat. Kul att ses!
Lena	Hej då, vi ses nog snart igen, nu när våren har kommit och man är ute mer!
Susanna	Javisst! Ha det bra, hej hej.

Jätte (*giant*) is used for emphasis: **jättestor** (**stor** = *big*). Illogically it is also used in **jätteliten** (**liten** = *small*).

2 Read the text or listen again and answer the questions.

a Where is Susanna's son during the day?
b Who takes him there, and who picks him up?
c Who is looking after Lena's children?
d Why can't Susanna have the same arrangement as Lena?

3 Match the Swedish to the English.

a	Hur mår du?	**1**	See you soon.
b	Det fungerar jättebra.	**2**	Now I have to go shopping for dinner.
c	Nu måste jag handla middagsmat.	**3**	Spring has arrived.
d	Vi ses nog snart igen.	**4**	How are you?
e	Våren har kommit.	**5**	It works fine.

4 What are the words used here for *days* **and** *cousins***? Do these plurals have the same endings?**

In some common words, the end consonant is dropped in daily speech. They include **jag** (*I*), **det** (*it*), **vad** (*what*), **och** (*and*), **är** (*am/are/is*, pronounced **e**).

Language discovery

1 NOUNS

There are five different plural endings for nouns in Swedish:

1 **-or**	**mamma/mammor**
2 **-ar**	**fru/fruar**
3 **-er, -r**	**kusin/kusiner, sko/skor**
4 **-n**	**äpple/äpplen**
5 **-0** (same in singular and plural)	**syskon/syskon**

Note that some words for family members have irregular plural forms:

moder (**mor**) becomes **två mödrar**

fader (**far**) becomes **två fäder**

broder (**bror**) becomes **två bröder**

and therefore we also get **mormödrar**, **morfäder**, **morbröder**, **farmödrar**, **farfäder**, **farbröder**.

(The plural of nouns is more fully explained in Unit 4.)

2 VOWELS

Vowels followed by one consonant or none are normally long. Vowels followed by two consonants or more are short.

hat	*hate*	**hatt**	*hat*
ko	*cow*	**konstig**	*strange*
ful	*ugly*	**full**	*full*
mål	*goal*	**mått**	*measure*
fin	*fine*	**finna**	*find*
het	*hot*	**hetta**	*heat*
sy	*sew*	**syster**	*sister*
kär	*dear*	**kärra**	*cart*
möta	*meet*	**mörker**	*darkness*

3 ANSWERING QUESTIONS

In affirmative answers, positive questions are answered with **ja**:

Är det kallt? (*Is it cold?*) **Ja, det är det.** (*Yes, it is.*)

Är Pelle din morbror? (*Is Pelle your uncle?*) **Ja, det är han.** (*Yes, he is.*)

In affirmative answers, negative questions (involving a *no*, *not*, etc.) are answered with **jo**:

Det är inte så kallt, eller hur? (*It isn't very cold, is it?*) **Jo, det är det.** (*Yes, it is.*)

Pelle är väl inte din morbror? (*Pelle is not your uncle, is he?*) **Jo, det är han.** (*Yes, he is.*)

Practice

1 **Consulting the table of plural endings, write the plural of the following nouns (clues are given in brackets as to which type of ending to use).**

a sko (3, shoe)
b familj (3)
c bi (4, bee)
d jobb (5)
e dag (2)
f krona (1)

2 02.03 **Listen and repeat the following sentences, observing the long and short vowels.**

a Jag hatar hattar.
b Hon möter mig i mörkret.
c En stor kopp kaffe och en kaka, tack!
d Lena och Lennart har fyra syskon.
e Vi vill ha vitt vin.
f Det är fullmåne en gång i månaden.

3 Give affirmative answers to these questions.

a Är det varmt på sommaren?
b Är det inte kallt på vintern?
c Är han inte din farbror?
d Är hon din faster?
e Är det mörkt på natten?
f Är det inte ljust på morgonen?

Pronunciation

The pronunciation of initial **g**, **k** and **sk** differs depending on what vowel follows. In front of **a**, **o**, **u**, **å** they are pronounced as written, but they are softened in front of **i**, **e**, **y**, **ä** and **ö**.

02.04 **Listen and repeat the following words.**

gul, göra, god, gymnastik, gift, gata, gåva, gäst, ge

kunskap, Kina, kedja, kall, kyla, köra, ko, källare, kål

skinn, skugga, sked, skära, skål, skylt, ska, skön

Conversation 2

02.05 **Listen to the words beginning with g, k or sk in this dialogue.**

Kerstin, skiing on a very cold day in winter, meets Göran.

How cold is it?

Kerstin	Hej Göran, det är skönt att åka skidor i dag. Jag gillar vintern!
Göran	Hej Kerstin. Det är kallt. Biter det inte i skinnet?
Kerstin	Jo, det är kyligt, minus tio grader. Vad gör du i morgon?
Göran	Om bilen startar kör jag till Göteborg. Kommer du med?
Kerstin	Det kan jag tyvärr inte, jag ska flyga via Kina till Nya Zeeland. Där är det sommar.

Speaking

02.06 **Play the part of Göran in this dialogue:**

Kerstin	Hej Göran, i dag biter det i skinnet.
Göran	Yes, it is cold, minus ten, but skiing is nice.
Kerstin	Ja, det är skönt. Vad gör du i morgon?
Göran	If I can start the car, I'll drive to Gothenburg. Will you come along?
Kerstin	Det kan jag inte, jag flyger till Kina och Nya Zeeland.

Reading

1 Read this summary of the first dialogue. Then answer the questions.

Susanna och Lena träffas utanför dagis. Det är länge sedan de sågs. Susanna har lämnat Pelle på dagis. Hennes man hämtar barnen där på eftermiddagen. Lena lämnar sina barn hos barnens morföräldrar och farföräldrar under veckan. Hon har tur som har släkten nära. Susanna ska handla middagsmat och sedan gå hem.

- **a** Var träffas Susanna och Lena?
- **b** Träffas de ofta?
- **c** Vad har Susanna gjort på dagis?
- **d** Var hämtar hennes man barnen på eftermiddagen?
- **e** Vad ska Susanna göra innan hon går hem?

2 Read the following description of a family and give the English equivalents for the words in bold.

Det här är min familj

Mor och far är mina **föräldrar**. Min mors föräldrar är min **mormor** och **morfar**. Min fars föräldrar är min **farmor** och **farfar**. Min mors **syskon** är min **moster** och **morbror**. Min fars syskon är min **faster** och **farbror**. Mina föräldrar har en **son** (det är jag, jag heter Adam) och en **dotter** (det är min syster Eva). Vi är syskon. Eva är min **syster** och jag är hennes **bror**. Vår moster och morbror har en dotter, det är vår **kusin** Lotta. Vår faster och farbror har en son, det är vår kusin Peter. Jag är gift med Elisabeth, det är min **fru**. Vi har en dotter som heter Ulrika. Min syster Eva är gift med Olav. Han är min **svåger** eftersom han är gift med min syster. Min fru Elisabeth är min syster Evas **svägerska** eftersom hon är gift med mig, Evas bror. De har en son som heter Jens. Ulrika och Jens är kusiner. Min kusin Peter har en dotter som heter Elin. Hon är **syssling** till Ulrika, vår dotter – **barn** till kusiner är sysslingar.

3 Answer the following questions.

a How is Adam related to Peter?
b How is Elisabeth related to Eva?
c How is Ulrika related to Jens?
d How is Elin related to Ulrika?
e How is Olav related to Adam?

Writing an e-mail

Unless you want to use abbreviations, there is not much difference between writing an e-mail and a letter. Normally you would start with a **Hej**, **Käre** (if you address it to a male friend), **Kära** (if it is a female, or plural), or simply **Käre vän/Kära vän/Kära vänner** (*Dear friend/s*). You finish with a **Hej då**, or with an even more familiar **Kram** (*Hug*), or **Ha det bra!** (*Take care!*), and your name, or you may end with a greeting to their wife, husband or family: **Hälsa din fru/man/familj**, or **Hälsa familjen!**

You will have some or all of these terms on your screen: **Skriv** (*Write*), **Till** (*To*), **Ämne** (*Subject*), **Kopia** (*Copy*), **Avbryt** (*Cancel*), **Skicka** (*Send*).

Write an e-mail to a friend, telling him or her about your family. Start it and conclude it in the way suggested.

- **a** Tell them about your grandparents and where they live.
- **b** Tell them about your siblings and their families.
- **c** Tell them what your children are called.

Test yourself

1 What are the five different plural endings of nouns? Can you form the plural of the following?

- **a** kusin
- **b** moder
- **c** syskon

2 What are the four seasons in Swedish?

3 Translate the following into Swedish:

- **a** We have relatives in America.
- **b** I am married to Eva. She is my wife.
- **c** Anna is my elder sister.

4 Answer the following questions.

- **a** Är det kallt?
- **b** Det är inte så kallt, eller hur?

SELF CHECK

	I CAN...
○	... describe my family.
○	... answer questions.
○	... talk about the seasons.
○	... form the plural of nouns.

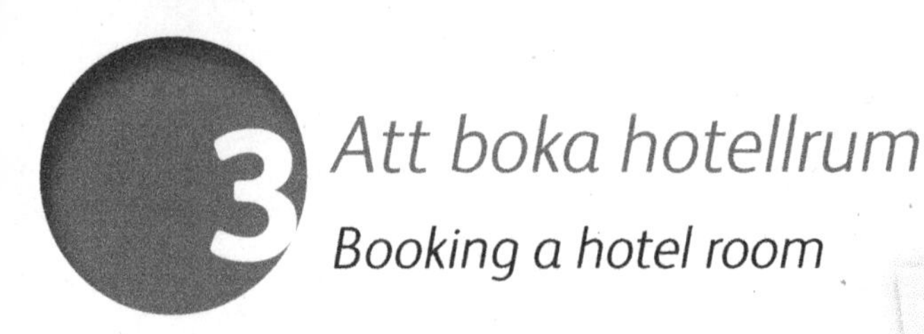

3 Att boka hotellrum

Booking a hotel room

In this unit you will learn how to:

- ***book a hotel room.***
- ***say days of the week and months of the year.***
- ***turn a statement into a question.***
- ***count to 100.***

CEFR: (A1) *Can handle numbers. Can indicate time by such phrases as last Friday and in November. Can get an idea of simpler informational material. Can fill in forms with personal details (name, address, registration) of yourself and others.*

Hotels in Sweden

You will be pleasantly surprised by the breakfast table in Swedish hotels. What they offer is normally much more than a continental breakfast, amounting to a slimmed down version of a **smörgåsbord**. In most if not all hotel rooms you will see a sign saying **rökning förbjuden** (*no smoking*). If you don't want to be disturbed, you hang a sign on your door handle: **Var god stör ej!** More affordable alternatives are **vandrarhem** (*hostels, backpackers*). The most popular one in Stockholm is the full-rigged steel ship Af Chapman, moored at Skeppsholmen island. If you prefer to holiday in the countryside, you can stay on a *farm* (**bo på lantgård**).

The terms below all relate to hotel facilities. Can you work out what they mean?

Rökfritt rum, **internetuppkoppling**, **telefonväckning**, **nattportier**, **luftkonditionering**.

Vocabulary builder

03.01 **Look at the words and fill in the missing translations. Then listen and try to imitate the pronunciation of the speakers.**

dubbelrum	*double room*
enkelrum	________
badrum	________
kontantbetalning	*cash payment*
kortbetalning	________
utforska	*explore*
reception	________
erbjuda	*offer*
utmärkt	*excellent*
utsikt	*view*
frukost	*breakfast*
resväska	*travel bag*
uppgift	*information*
nyckel	*key*
vistelse	*stay*
hiss	*elevator, lift*

NEW EXPRESSIONS

Look at the words and expressions that are used in the following conversation. Note their meanings.

Hur låter det?	*How does that sound?*
Går det bra?	*Is that OK?*
Då säger vi så.	*OK, agreed.*
Får jag be...	*May I ask…*
äktenskap	*marriage*
lejon	*lion*
häftig	*cool*

Conversation 1

03.02 *Emma and Erik look for a hotel in Stockholm. When they've found one, they check in.*

1 What do they discover at the hotel check-in?

Erik	Jaha, nu är vi här! Nu ska vi utforska Stockholm under en hel sommarvecka mitt i juli!
Emma	Ja, men först måste vi hitta ett trevligt hotell.
Erik	Titta där! 'TVÅ LEJON', ett sånt (sådant) häftigt namn!
Emma	Det verkar bra, vi går in.
(vid receptionen):	
Emma	God dag, vi vill gärna boka rum för två vuxna för sex dagar, från i dag som är tisdag till nästa måndag. Söndag är sista natten.
Portiern	Jaha, då ska vi se vad vi kan erbjuda. Dubbelrum med utsikt över Gamla Stan (staden), eget badrum, hur låter det?
Emma	Alldeles utmärkt! Är frukosten inkluderad?
Portiern	Ja, frukosten är inkluderad.
Erik	Hur mycket kostar det?
Portiern	Det kostar 780 kronor per natt. Juni, juli, augusti och september är högsäsong.
Erik	Hur dags är incheckning och när måste vi checka ut?
Portiern	Ni kan checka in från klockan 12, och vi har alltid sen utcheckning, också klockan 12. Och behöver ni lämna resväskorna efter utcheckning så har vi ett säkert bagage-rum.
Emma	Vi har ett litet barnbarn, en sondotter, som kanske sover över någon natt, går det bra?
Portiern	Javisst, hur gammal är hon?
Emma	Hon är fem år.
Portiern	Då tar vi inte alls betalt för henne. Hon är så välkommen!
Emma	Tack, då säger vi så. Vi tar rummet och checkar in nu direkt.
Portiern	Då får jag be er fylla i lite uppgifter här. Varsågod.

2 What do you think? Read the conversation and answer the questions.

a How many days are they staying in Stockholm?

b What time can they check in and when do they have to check out?

c Apart from Emma and Erik, who might use the room?

3 Match the questions and answers.

a Hur mycket kostar rummet?

b Är frukosten inkluderad?

c Vad kan man se från dubbelrummet?

d Hur gammalt är barnbarnet?

e När checkar de in?

1 De checkar in direkt.

2 Hon är fem år.

3 Det kostar 780 kronor.

4 Frukosten är inkluderad.

5 Dubbelrummet har utsikt över Gamla Stan.

4 How does Emma ask if breakfast is included? What answer does she get?

5 How does Erik say the following? Where does the verb appear in each phrase?

a Now we are here.

b Now we shall explore Stockholm.

Language discovery

1 STATEMENTS

Hon är fem år. Är hon fem år?

The first sentence is a statement while the second is a question.

Statements have normal word order: noun + verb/subject + predicate. Questions have inverted word order: verb + noun/predicate + subject. This is also the case when it starts with a question word: **Hur gammal är hon?**

2 WORD ORDER

Nu är vi här. Då tar vi inte betalt.

If a sentence starts with an adverb, the word order is inverted.

3 NUMBERS TO 100

03.03 Here are the numbers up to 100. Listen for the correct pronunciation.

1 **en, ett**	11 **elva**	20 **tjugo** (**tjuge**)
2 **två**	12 **tolv**	21 **tjugoen** (**tjuen**)
3 **tre**	12 **tretton**	30 **trettio** (**tretti**)
4 **fyra**	14 **fjorton**	40 **fyrtio** (**förti**)
5 **fem**	15 **femton**	50 **femtio** (**femti**)
6 **sex**	16 **sexton**	60 **sextio** (**sexti**)
7 **sju**	17 **sjutton**	70 **sjuttio** (**sjutti**)
8 **åtta**	18 **arton**	80 **åttio** (**åtti**)
9 **nio** (pronounced **nie**)	19 **nitton**	90 **nittio** (**nitti**)
10 **tio** (**tie**)		100 **hundra**, **ett hundra**

When working with numbers, the following terms are used.

Addition:

5 + 5 = 10 (**fem plus fem är lika med tio**)

Subtraktion:

20 – 10 = 10 (**tjugo minus tio är lika med tio**)

Multiplikation:

2 x 5 = 10 (**två gånger fem är lika med tio**)

Division:

50 ÷ 5 = 10 (**femtio delat med fem är lika med tio**)

4 DAYS AND MONTHS

03.04 The days of the week are (no capital letters unless starting a sentence):

måndag, tisdag, onsdag, torsdag, fredag, lördag och söndag

Jag är på kontoret från måndag morgon till fredag eftermiddag. (*I am at the office from Monday morning until Friday afternoon.*)

The months of the year are (no capital letters unless starting a sentence):

januari, **februari**, **mars**, **april**, **maj**, **juni**, **juli**, **augusti**, **september**, **oktober**, **november och december**

Jag arbetar från vecka två i januari till slutet av juni, och från början av augusti till mitten av december. (*I work from the second week of January until the end of June, and from the beginning of August until mid-December.*)

LANGUAGE TIP

The preposition **i** and an added **-s** is used when speaking about a day that has just passed: **i måndags, i fredags**. The preposition **på** is used when speaking about a day that will soon come: **på tisdag, på lördag**.

I fredags var jag sjuk men på måndag är jag säkert frisk igen. (*Last Friday I was ill but I will surely be well again on Monday.*)

LANGUAGE TIP

A peculiarity with Swedish is the way in which it refers to the number of the week in the calendar, rather than stating dates:

Jag åker skidor vecka sex (*I go skiing in week six*); **Jag är i Köpenhamn vecka tjugo** (*I will be in Copenhagen in week twenty*); **Jag har semester vecka trettiotre** (*I am on holiday in week thirty-three*).

Practice

1 Turn the following statements into questions.

- **a** Vi går in.
- **b** Vi har alltid sen utcheckning.
- **c** Det kostar 780 kronor.

Turn the following questions into statements.

- **d** Går det bra?
- **e** Ingår frukost?
- **f** Är hon fem år?

2 Change the word order in the following sentences by starting them with nu (*now*) or då (*then*).

- **a** Vi tar rummet.
- **b** Hon är så välkommen.
- **c** De utforskar Stockholm.
- **d** Han vill lämna resväskorna.
- **e** Du måste hitta ett trevligt hotell.
- **f** Jag ska se vad jag kan erbjuda.

3 Read out the following and give the answers.

- **a** 15 + 35 =
- **b** 100 – 40 =
- **c** 5 x 15 =
- **d** 100 ÷ 4 =

När är du född? (*When were you born?*) Note that English uses past tense, Swedish present tense.

4 **What month and what day is your birthday? On what day of the week is it this year?**

Two of the days in the week are named after the Nordic gods Oden and Tor, one after the goddess Frigga or Freya, and one after the moon. Which are the weekdays?

Speaking

03.05 **Play the part of the desk clerk in this conversation.**

Emma	Kan vi boka ett dubbelrum?
Desk clerk	*Yes, we have a double room with a view of Gamla Stan.*
Erik	Hur mycket kostar det?
Desk clerk	*It will be 780 kronor.*
Emma	Var är hissen?
Desk clerk	*The lift is over there to the right.*
Erik	På vilken våning är rummet?
Desk clerk	*The room is on the first floor.*

Pronunciation

03.06 **Listen and repeat the following. What is the advantage of having relatives in Lund and Stockholm?**

Min kusin Ulla är professor i kemi på Lunds universitet. När hon är i Stockholm på konferens bor hon hos oss. När vi är i Lund bor vi hos henne och hennes man Torsten som är bankman. Då är vi deras gäster (guests). Vi får en nyckel så att vi kan komma och gå som vi vill. Det är bra. Det är gratis för dem att bo i Stockholm och för oss i Lund.

Conversation 2

03.07 *Emma and Erik fill in the form that the desk clerk gives them.*

1 What personal information are they asked to give?

Erik	Aha, namn, nationalitet, hemadress, telefonnummer, vi sätter oss där borta i soffan och gör det.
Emma	Sådär. Namn: Nilsson-Pedersen.
Erik	Nationalitet: ja, blandäktenskap...svensk och dansk.
Emma	Hemadress: Storgatan 77, Malmö.
Erik	Telefon, det är väl enklast att ta mobilnumret: 070-12 34 567 (noll-sju-noll-ett-två-tre-fyra-fem-sex-sju, or noll-sjuttio-tolv-trettifyra-femhundrasextisju). Och datum för vår bokning: 14 mars till 21 mars Det skulle väl vara allt. Varsågod.
Portiern	Tack för det. Här är nycklarna till rummet, hissen är där borta till höger, rummet är på andra våningen. Behöver ni hjälp med väskorna?
Emma	Nej tack, det klarar vi själva. Hur dags serveras frukosten i morgon?
Portiern	Den serveras mellan klockan sju och tio.
Emma	Tack. Jag glömde säga till om icke-rökare.
Portiern	Alla våra rum har rökförbud, liksom restaurangen.
Erik	Bra, tack, då åker vi upp och installerar oss.
Portiern	Välkomna, och jag hoppas ni får en trevlig vistelse i Stockholm.

2 Find the expressions in the conversation that mean the following:

a mixed marriage
b that should be all
c the elevator/lift is over there on the right
d all rooms are non-smoking
e I hope you have a nice time in Stockholm

webpage

www.webpagerealia.com

Alla rum på hotellet har TV och internetuppkoppling. Möblerna i hotellet är i skandinavisk formgivning. Matsalen har utsikt mot vattnet. Restaurangen har fem stjärnor i Guide Michelin. Hotellet har motionsrum, bastu och simbassäng.

Reading

1 Read this advertisement. Can you guess what the following words mean:

a uppkoppling
b formgivning
c stjärna
d bastu

2 Now answer these questions.

a What is included in all rooms?
b Where was the furniture designed?
c What can be seen from the dining room?
d How can you keep in good physical shape at this hotel?

Writing

Fill in this hotel registration form:

Förnamn: ____________ Efternamn: ____________

Hemadress: ____________

Nationalitet: ____________

Telefonnummer och/eller mobilnummer: ____________

Antal vuxna: ____________ Antal barn under 18 år: ____________

Datum för incheckning: ________ Datum för utcheckning: ________

Speciella önskemål (special requirements): ____________

Väckning (wake-up call): ____________ Tvätt (laundry): ________

Test yourself

1 Translate the following sentences into Swedish:

a I go to Stockholm on Thursday.

b He books a hotel room from Wednesday to Sunday.

c My daughter arrives on Tuesday.

2 Write the sentences below in Swedish using words for the numbers rather than figures.

a Coffee is 15 and a cake is 6, that's 21 kronor.

b My phone number is 57 63 28.

c The country code for Sweden is 0046.

3 Turn these statements in English into questions in Swedish.

a Ebba is a chemistry professor.

b She stays with us when she is in Lund.

c We are their guests.

d It is free for her to stay with us.

SELF CHECK

	I CAN...
○	**... check in at a hotel.**
○	**... say the days of the week and months of the year.**
○	**... turn a statement into a question.**
○	**... count up to 100.**

R1 Review 1

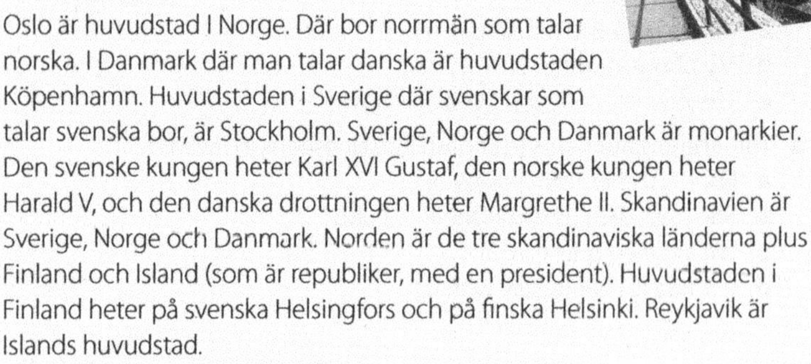

1 Read the following text, then answer the questions:

Oslo är huvudstad I Norge. Där bor norrmän som talar norska. I Danmark där man talar danska är huvudstaden Köpenhamn. Huvudstaden i Sverige där svenskar som talar svenska bor, är Stockholm. Sverige, Norge och Danmark är monarkier. Den svenske kungen heter Karl XVI Gustaf, den norske kungen heter Harald V, och den danska drottningen heter Margrethe II. Skandinavien är Sverige, Norge och Danmark. Norden är de tre skandinaviska länderna plus Finland och Island (som är republiker, med en president). Huvudstaden i Finland heter på svenska Helsingfors och på finska Helsinki. Reykjavik är Islands huvudstad.

- **a** Which are the Scandinavian countries?
- **b** Which are the Nordic countries?
- **c** Which of them are republics?
- **d** Which are monarchies?
- **e** What are the five Nordic capitals called?

2 In Swedish, how do you tell apart your aunts, uncles and grandparents on your mother's side of the family from those on your father's?

3 03.08 **Sofia from Sweden and Ivan from Russia (who is better at languages than geography) get to know each other online. This is their first chat.**

Read it and answer the questions that follow.

Sofia	Hej, det här är Sofia! Vem är du?
Ivan	God dag Sofia. Jag heter Ivan. Jag är ryss och bor i Moskva. Var bor du?
Sofia	Jag bor i Malmö.
Ivan	Var ligger Malmö? Är det en stor stad?
Sofia	Malmö är en stad i Sverige. Vad jobbar du med?
Ivan	Jag studerar fortfarande. Jag läser medicin och ska blir doktor. Här i Moskva bor elva miljoner.

Sofia	Oj då, Moskva är en storstad och Malmö en liten stad. Hur gammal är du?
Ivan	Jag är 26 år nu. Hur gammal är du?
Sofia	Jag är 24, och jag är sjuksköterska. Har du några syskon?
Ivan	Ja, jag har två bröder här i Moskva, både en storebror och en lillebror. Andrej som är 30 och Alexander som är 23. Och har du några syskon?
Sofia	Här i Malmö är vi också tre syskon: jag själv, min storasyster Rebecka som är 27 och min lillasyster Pernilla som är 19 och yngst. Vad heter dina föräldrar?
Ivan	Min mor heter Ludmilla och är ingenjör och min far heter Aleksej och är professor i nordiska språk vid universitetet. Det är därför jag är intresserad av svenska. Och dina föräldrar?
Sofia	Min mamma Erika är flygkapten och flyger ofta till Ryssland, och min pappa Olle är atomfysiker. Hon är 56 och han 58.
Ivan	Så trevligt att träffa dig på nätet, jag hoppas att vi snart kan träffas här i Moskva eller i Malmö.
Sofia	Du flyger till Köpenhamn och tar sedan tåget direkt från flygplatsen, Kastrup, till Malmö, över Öresundsbron, det tar bara femton minuter. Hej då.
Ivan	Adjö så länge.

a Where do Sofia and her sisters live? And Ivan and his brothers?
b What is Sofia's job? What will Ivan be, once he has finished his studies?
c What are their parents' occupations?
d What is the Copenhagen Airport called, and how do you get from there to Malmö?

4 Looking at the conversation, write in words the age of Sofia, her sisters and her parents, and of Ivan and his brothers.

5 How can you tell by Ivan's greetings that he is slightly more formal than Sofia?

På shoppingrunda

Out shopping

In this unit, you will learn how to

- ***ask for sizes and colours when buying clothes.***
- ***say numbers from 100 onwards.***
- ***find out how much things cost.***
- ***use the definite form of nouns.***

CEFR: (A1) *Can understand and use familiar everyday expressions and very basic phrases.* **(A2)** *Can use simple descriptive language to make brief statements about and compare objects and possessions.*

Paying

Before shopping, you can withdraw **pengar** (*money*) from **en uttagsautomat** (*cash machine*) or pay with your **kreditkort** (*credit card*) with its **kod** (*pin number*). If you pay **kontant** (*cash*), you need either **sedlar** (*bank notes*) or **mynt** (*coins*). The Swedish currency is **kronor** and **ören**. The bank notes are 20 kr, 50 kr, 100 kr, 500 kr and 1000 kr. Coins are 1, 5 and 10 kronor.

These are the instructions on the cashpoint screen when you withdraw money. What is the machine telling you to do?

Välkommen

Sätt in ditt kort

Tryck din kod

Välj belopp

Tryck UTTAG

Tag ditt kort

Tag pengarna

Välkommen åter

Vocabulary builder

04.01 **Look at the words and phrases and complete the missing English equivalents. Then listen and imitate the pronunciation of the speakers as closely as possible.**

COLOURS

svart	*black*
vit	*white*
grå	*grey*
grön	______
röd	______
gul	*yellow*
blå	______
brun	______
orange	______
rosa	*pink*

CLOTHES

kläder	*clothes*
skor	*shoes*
stövlar	*boots*
skjorta	*shirt*
slips	*tie*
kjol	*skirt*
klänning	*dress*
rock	*coat*
byxor	*trousers*
kavaj	*jacket*
tröja	*sweater, cardigan*
hatt	______
halsduk	*scarf*
bälte	______
strumpor	*stockings, socks*

TYPES OF SHOPS

affär	*shop*
apotek	*pharmacy, chemist's*
varuhus	*department store*
-handel	*shop suffix, as in* **blomsterhandel**, **bokhandel**, **järnhandel** (*hardware*)
torg	*market*
saluhall	*food hall*
bageri	________
systembolag	*state-run off licence / state liquor store*

IN THE SHOP

handla, köpa	*buy*
kvitto	*receipt*
byta	*change*
prislapp	________
livsmedel	*food*
disk	*desk, counter*
Kan jag få se på?	*May I have a look at that?*
Kan jag få prova?	*May I try?*
för stor	*too big*
för liten	*too small*
Kläderna passar bra.	*The clothes fit well.*
Tack, det tar jag.	*Thanks, I'll take that.*
lagom	*exactly right*

NEW EXPRESSIONS

Klappat och klart.	*All fixed and done.*
Hänger du med?	*Want to come along?*

Conversation 1

04.02 *Lena discovers how worn Fredrik's shoes are. When they are walking in the city, they happen to pass a shoe shop. They enter, and she talks him into buying a new pair of shoes.*

1 How can you tell that she is more keen than he is?

Lena	Du behöver verkligen nya skor, Fredrik!
Fredrik	Men du vet hur trist jag tycker det är att handla kläder!
Lena	Jag vet, men det måste du göra i alla fall. Här är en bra skoaffär. Nu går vi in!
Expediten	Välkomna, vad kan jag hjälpa till med?
Lena	Min man behöver nya promenadskor, gärna bruna, och i storlek 45.
Expediten	Det visar jag så gärna. Varsågod och sitt så länge så ska jag plocka fram.
Lena	Se inte så arg ut, Fredrik! Prova det här paret, de ser bekväma ut.

Fredrik knyter på sig skorna och vandrar runt i affären. Lena frågar honom:

Lena	Hur känns de?
Fredrik	Jodå, de känns faktiskt bra. Rätt storlek, och jag gillar färgen. Dem tar vi.
Lena	Men ska du inte prova några andra alls?
Fredrik	Nej, de här är perfekta! Hur mycket kostar de?
Expediten	De kostar 750 kronor. Spara kvittot, ni har en veckas bytesrätt.
Fredrik	Tack för det. Klappat och klart, nu går vi, Lena!

2 Read the conversation and answer the questions.

a Why is Fredrik unwilling to buy shoes?
b What kind of shoes does he need? Which colour? Which size?
c How many pair of shoes does he try on?
d Why should you hang on to the receipt?

3 Find the following nouns in the dialogue: *shoes, clothes, shoe shop, receipt.*

4 Match the questions and the answers.

a Jag tycker det är trist.	**1** Please sit down.
b Se inte så arg ut.	**2** I'd be happy to show you what we have.
c Varsågod och sitt.	**3** I dislike.
d De känns faktiskt bra.	**4** Don't look so angry.
e Det visar jag så gärna.	**5** They actually feel comfortable.

Language discovery

1 GENDER OF NOUNS

Nouns are either non-neuter (mainly living creatures) such as **en man, en kvinna, en katt, en hund** or neuter (generally inanimate things) such as **ett hus, ett land**. There are, however, some exceptions to the rule, for example **ett barn** (*child*), **ett djur** (*animal*), **ett lejon, en stad** (*city*), **en sjö** (*lake*).

2 PLURAL OF NOUNS

These are the basic rules (there are exceptions):

- Nouns in the first group (plural **-or**) are non-neuter, ending in **-a** in the singular which is dropped in the plural: **en flicka flera flickor, en soffa flera soffor**. This is the biggest group.
- Nouns in the second group (plural **-ar**) are also non-neuter, the singular often ending in **-e, -el, -en, -er** (where the **-e** is dropped in the plural), **-ing** or **-ning**: **en pojke flera pojkar, en tidning flera tidningar**. Many are one-syllable words: **en stol flera stolar**. Two words change their vowels: **en dotter flera döttrar, en mor (moder) flera mödrar**.
- Nouns in the third group (plural **-er** or **-r**) are either non-neuter (most of them) or neuter (a few). Many are borrowed from other languages and are often stressed on the last syllable: **en intervju flera intervjuer, ett kafé flera kaféer**. Nouns taking the plural ending **-r** are mainly non-neuter, ending in a vowel in the singular: **en sko flera skor, en ko flera kor**. Some change their vowel: **en hand flera händer, en son flera söner**.
- Nouns in the fourth group (plural **-n**) are all neuter, ending in a vowel in the singular: **ett äpple flera äpplen, ett foto flera foton**.
- Nouns in the fifth group are mainly neuter ending in a consonant in the singular, but also non-neuter denoting persons and ending in **-are, -ande** and **-er** in the singular. They have no plural ending: **ett hus flera hus, ett språk flera språk, en stockholmare flera stockholmare, en studerande flera studerande, en musiker flera musiker**. This is the second biggest group.

Thus most non-neuter nouns belong to group one, two or three with **-or, -ar, -er/-r** in the plural, and most neutral nouns belong to group four or five with **-n** or no ending in the plural.

3 DEFINITE ARTICLE WITH NOUNS

The definite article of nouns in the singular is **-en**, **-n**, **-et** and **-t**, attached to the end of the word: **mannen**, **kvinnan**, **katten**, **hunden**, **huset**, **landet**, **barnet**, **djuret**, **lejonet**, **staden**, **sjön**.

The definite article of plural nouns is mostly either **-en** or **-na**: **männen**, **kvinnorna**.

4 NUMBERS ABOVE 100

04.03 We have already learned how to count to 100. Now we will look at numbers over 100.

101 (**etthundraen**), 212 (**tvåhundratolv**), 323 (**trehundratjugotre**), 434 (**fyrahundratrettiofyra**), 545 (**femhundrafyrtiofem**), 656 (**sexhundrafemtiosex**), 767 (**sjuhundrasextiosju**), 878 (**åttahundrasjuttioåtta**), 989 (**niohundraåttionio**), 1001 (**ett tusen ett**), 2560 (**tvåtusenfemhundrasextio**)

Years (**årtal**): 1668 (**sextonhundrasextioåtta**), 1812 (**artonhundratolv**), 1917 (**nittonhundrasjutton**), 2014 (**tjugohundrafjorton**, or **tvåtusenfjorton**)

Practice

1 **Which of the following nouns are non-neuter, and which ones neuter?**

dag, katt, lejon, hund, djur, rum, stearinljus

2 **Change each of the nouns given above from the indefinite to the definite form, in singular and plural. The first one has been done for you.**

dag – dagen – dagar – dagarna

3 **Turn these singular nouns into plural ones.**

kvinna, möbel, tändsticka, smycke, bok, sko, bi, man

4 If a woman wears a medium size in dresses and shoes, which sizes should she ask for in Sweden? And a man? Write the sizes in words rather than figures.

A condensed chart of clothing sizes in Sweden appears below (British and American equivalents within brackets).

Ladies: S – 36–8 (10–12, 6–8), M – 40–2 (14–16, 10–12), L 44–6 (18–20, 14–16), XL 48–50 (22–4, 18–20)

Men: S – 50–2 (40–2, 40–1), M – 54–6 (44–6), L – 58 (48), for shirts: S – 39–40 (15.5–16), M – 41–2 (16.5–17), L – 43 (17.5)

Men's shoes: 38 (5, 6), 40 (6.5, 7.5) 42 (7.5, 8.5), 44 (9.5, 10.5)

Ladies' shoes: 35 (2.5, 5), 36 (3.5, 6), 37 (4, 6.5), 38 (5, 7.5), etc.

Speaking

04.04 **Listen to the conversation once more, then play the part of Jenny in this dialogue.**

Sofia	Jag behöver faktiskt titta på lite nya kläder.
Jenny	*We'll start in the big shopping centre, there are lots to choose from.*
Sofia	Den här sitter snyggt. Vad tycker du?
Jenny	*Great! Have you got matching shoes?*

Pronunciation

04.05 In 2013, Barnbidraget, the state child benefit, amounted to 1050 kr tax free per month. Listen and repeat the list of clothes that Susanna bought for Pelle with the allowance.

Ett par stövlar	140 kr
En tröja	90 kr
En jacka	275 kr
En halsduk	30 kr
Ett par byxor	180 kr
Tre par strumpor à	25 kr, 75 kr
Ett par skor	260 kr
Summa:	1050 kr

VOCABULARY

04.06

kolla	*look at, check it out*
häftig	*smart*
prick	*dot*
provrum	*changing room*
väska	*bag, suitcase*
klack	*heel*
nöjd	*satisfied, content*
slapp (past tense of **slippa**)	*escaped, avoided*
otäck	*nasty*
smakråd	*giving good advice*

Conversation 2

04.07 *On a drab day, Jenny and Sofia escape the rain by going into a big shopping centre.*

1 What are they looking for? What do they end up buying?

Jenny	Hej, Sofia, usch en sån trist och regnig dag! Häng med på en shoppingrunda!
Sofia	OK, här finns mycket att välja på.
Jenny	Titta, den här klänningen ser väl häftig ut! Svart, med vita prickar, lite klassisk. Ska du prova?
Sofia	Jag tar en i storlek 38 till provrummet.
Jenny	Jag provar långbyxor under tiden, och en matchande tröja.
Sofia	Jättebra, passar precis till dina stövlar och din vinterkappa. Min klänning sitter snyggt, eller hur?
Jenny	Absolut! Har du skor som passar till?
Sofia	Ja, mina svarta med halvhög klack blir perfekta.
Jenny	Så bra. Du köper klänningen, jag köper byxorna och tröjan. Är vi nöjda för idag?
Sofia	Det tycker jag. Nu behöver vi en kopp kaffe efter våra fantastiska fynd!
Jenny	Tänk sån tur vi hade, vi fick dessutom tjugo procents rabatt och full returrätt i en vecka!
Sofia	Och så slapp vi vara ute i det otäcka vädret. Tack för att du följde med som smakråd!

2 Find the expressions in the conversation that mean the following:

- **a** black, with white dots
- **b** It is a nice fit.
- **c** We got a discount today.
- **d** We avoided the horrible weather.

3 Match the questions and answers.

a	Jag provar långbyxor under tiden.	**1**	We were lucky.
b	Det finns mycket att välja på.	**2**	I'll try on some trousers in the meantime.
c	Den passar precis till dina stövlar.	**3**	Is that it for today?
d	Är vi nöjda för i dag?	**4**	There is a lot to choose from.
e	Tänk sån (sådan) tur vi hade.	**5**	It matches your boots perfectly.

Reading

The black dress that Sofia bought has a fabric label with washing instructions (tvättråd). How should it be washed?

Material: 60 % linne (*linen*), 40 % bomull (*cotton*)

Tvättråd: Tvätta i högst 40 grader för hand eller i maskin. Tvätta med liknande (*similar*) färger. Kemtvätt (kemisk tvätt = *dryclean*) rekommenderas. Får ej (*must not*) torktumlas, endast (*only*) dropptorkas.

Candles (**stearinljus**) light up the long dark winter evenings. In the month leading up to *Christmas* (**jul**), the four candles in an *advent candle holder* (**adventsljusstake**) are lit, one each Sunday. By *Christmas Eve* (**julafton**) all four candles are burning, at different heights. Sweden is well known for its design in *furniture* (**möbler**), textiles, glass, ceramics, *wood* (**trä**), *stationery* (**pappersvaror**), etc. If you visit Sweden, you might want to bring back some souvenirs, like the red wooden horse from the province of *Dalecarlia* (**dalahäst**) and other *folk art* (**hemslöjd**), *safety matches* (**säkerhetständstickor**), candles, *table runners* (**bordslöpare**), glass, *crystal vases* (**kristallvaser**) and *silver jewellery* (**silversmycken**).

Writing

1 **It is your last day in Sweden. Write a list of souvenirs you want to take home for family and friends.**

2 **Swedish winters can be bitterly cold. Write a shopping list in Swedish of some warm clothing that you need, also stating your size and your favourite colours.**

> **NAMES**
>
> Swedes not only celebrate birthdays, but also *namedays* (**namnsdagar**). Every day in the calendar, with few exceptions for the major holidays, carries a first name, often two that are similar and/or female and male varieties of the same name. **Fruntimmersveckan** in late July, starting with Sara and ending with Kristina and Kerstin, is exclusively a woman's week (though one day short). You can see a name day calendar on pages 44 and 45.

Test yourself

1 What do the following expressions mean?
- **a** Betala kontant.
- **b** Använda kreditkortet.
- **c** Ta ut pengar i bankautomaten.
- **d** Använda sedlar och mynt.

2 Say the following in Swedish:
- **a** I would like to try on a pair of trousers.
- **b** I like the light blue colour.
- **c** How much are they?
- **d** Can I pay by credit card?

3 Give the Swedish for each of the following:
- **a** You really need new shoes.
- **b** Buying clothes is boring.
- **c** Right size, and I like the colour.
- **d** Aren't you going to try on some more?

SELF CHECK

	I CAN...
○	... ask about sizes, colours and prices.
○	... write a shopping list.
○	... count from 100 to 1000.

	January	February	March	April	May
1	Nyårsdagen	Max	Albin	Harald	Valborg
2	Svea	Kyndelsmässodagen	Ernst	Gudmund	Filip
3	Alfred	Disa	Gunborg	Ferdinand	Göta
4	Rut	Ansgar	Adrian	Ambrosius	Monika
5	Hanna	Agata	Tora	Nanna	Gotthard
6	Trettondedag jul	Dorotea	Ebba	Vilhelm	Sigmund
7	August	Rikard	Ottilia	Ingemund	Gustava
8	Erland	Berta	Filippa	Hemming	Åke
9	Gunnar	Fanny	Torbjörn	Otto	Jonatan
10	Sigurd	Eugenia	Ethel	Ingvar	Esbjörn
11	Hugo	Yngve	Edvin	Ulf	Märta
12	Frideborg	Evelina	Viktoria	Julius	Carlos
13	Knut	Agne	Greger	Artur	Linnea
14	Felix	Valentin	Matilda	Tiburtius	Halvard
15	Laura	Sigfrid	Kristoffer	Olivia	Sofia
16	Hjalmar	Julia	Herbert	Patrik	Hilma
17	Anton	Alexandra	Gertrud	Elias	Rebecka
18	Hilda	Frida	Edvard	Valdemar	Erik
19	Henrik	Gabriella	Josef	Olaus Petri	Alrik
20	Fabian	Hulda	Joakim	Amalia	Karolina
21	Agnes	Hilding	Bengt	Anselm	Konstantin
22	Vincent	Martina	Viktor	Albertina	Henning
23	Emilia	Torsten	Gerda	Georg	Desideria
24	Erika	Mattias	Gabriel	Vega	Ragnvald
25	Paulus	Sigvard	Marie bebådelsedag	Markus	Urban
26	Botilda	Torgny	Emanuel	Teresia	Vilhelmina
27	Göte	Lage	Rudolf	Engelbrekt	Blenda
28	Karl	Maria	Malkolm	Ture	Ingeborg
29	Valter		Jonas	Tyko	Baltsar
30	Gunhild		Holger	Mariana	Fritjof
31	Ivar		Ester		Isabella

	June	July	August	September	October	November	December
1	Nikodemus	Aron	Per	Samuel	Ragnar	Allhelgonadagen	Oskar
2	Rutger	Rosa	Karin	Justus	Ludvig	Tobias	Beata
3	Ingemar	Aurora	Tage	Alfhild	Evald	Hubert	Lydia
4	Holmfrid	Ulrika	Arne	Moses	Frans	Sverker	Barbro
5	Bo	Melker	Ulrik	Adela	Bror	Eugen	Sven
6	Gustav	Esaias	Sixten	Sakarias	Jenny	Gustav Adolf	Nikolaus
7	Robert	Klas	Arnold	Regina	Birgitta	Ingegerd	Agaton
8	Salomon	Kjell	Sylvia	Alma	Nils	Vendela	Virginia
9	Börje	Götilda	Roland	Augusta	Ingrid	Teodor	Anna
10	Svante	Anund	Lars	Tord	Helmer	Martin Luther	Malin
11	Bertil	Eleonora	Susanna	Dagny	Erling	Mårten	Daniel
12	Eskil	Herman	Klara	Tyra	Valfrid	Konrad	Alexander
13	Aina	Joel	Hillevi	Ambjörn	Teofil	Kristian	Lucia
14	Håkan	Folke	Ebbe	Ida	Manfred	Emil	Sten
15	Justina	Ragnhild	Stella	Sigrid	Hedvig	Leopold	Gottfrid
16	Axel	Reinhold	Brynolf	Eufemia	Finn	Edmund	Assar
17	Torborg	Alexis	Verner	Hildegard	Antoinetta	Napoleon	Inge
18	Björn	Fredrik	Helena	Alvar	Lukas	Magnhild	Abraham
19	Germund	Sara	Magnus	Fredrika	Tore	Elisabet	Isak
20	Flora	Margareta	Bernhard	Agda	Sibylla	Pontus	Israel
21	Alf	Johanna	Josefina	Matteus	Birger	Helga	Tomas
22	Paulina	Magdalena	Henrietta	Maurits	Seved	Cecilia	Natalie
23	Adolf	Emma	Signe	Tekla	Sören	Klemens	Adam
24	Johannes Döparens dag	Kristina	Bartolomeus	Gerhard	Evert	Gudrun	Eva
25	David	Jakob	Lovisa	Signild	Inga	Katarina	Juldagen
26	Rakel	Jesper	Östen	Enar	Amanda	Torkel	Stefan
27	Selma	Marta	Rolf	Dagmar	Sabina	Astrid	Johannes
28	Leo	Botvid	Augustin	Lennart	Simon	Malte	Menlösa barns dag
29	Petrus	Olof	Hans	Mikael	Viola	Sune	Abel
30	Elof	Algot	Albert	Helge	Elsa	Anders	Set
31		Elin	Arvid		Edit		Sylvester

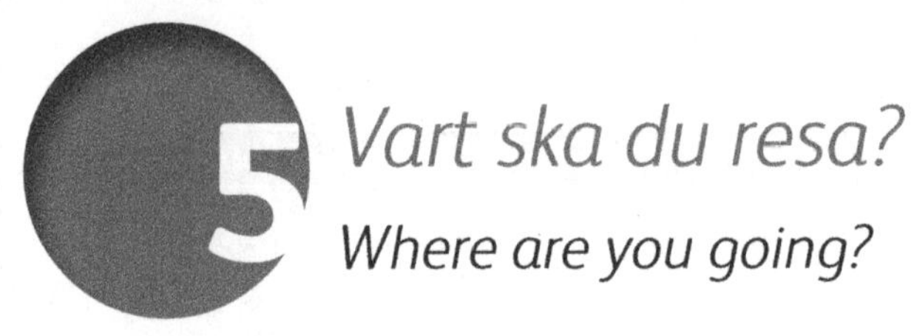

5 Vart ska du resa?

Where are you going?

In this unit, you will learn how to:

- ***plan a journey.***
- ***buy a ticket.***
- ***ask and tell the time.***
- ***give directions.***

CEFR: (A1) *Can get simple information about travel, use of public transport, give directions and buy tickets. Can write short, simple notes. Can find specific, predictable information in simple everyday material such as timetables.*

Travelling in Sweden

Sweden from north to south is close to 1600 kilometres and from west to east almost 500 kilometres. Travelling is fast and efficient, by **bil** (*car*), by **tåg** (*train*), by **färja** or **båt** (*boat*) or by **flyg** (*plane*). You can book your tickets online or buy them in a **biljettautomat** (*ticket machine*) at the train station and the airport, or directly over the **biljettköp** (*counter*). You can also **hyra en bil** (*hire a car*). Roads outside the main cities are normally uncluttered. The **högsta fartgräns** (*speed limit*) on a **motorväg** (*motorway*) is **110** or **120 kilometer i timmen** (*68–74 mph*), in cities normally **50 km i timmen** (*30 mph*) or less. On 3 September 1967, traffic switched from **vänstertrafik** (*driving on the left*) to **högertrafik** (*driving on the right*).

Read the following. Why do you have to pay congestion charges if you want to drive into Stockholm in the daytime?

Det finns många bilar i Stockholm men inte tillräckligt många parkeringsplatser. Luften (the air) blir också bättre med mindre trafik.

Därför måste man betala en trängselskatt om man vill köra i centrala Stockholm på dagen.

Vocabulary builder

05.01 **Look at the words and phrases and complete the missing English equivalents. Then listen and imitate the pronunciation of the speakers as closely as possible.**

PLANNING A TRIP

enkel biljett	*single ticket*
en returbiljett	______
resebyrå	*travel agency*
en resebyråman/kvinna	______
tidtabell	*timetable*
fönsterplats	*window seat*
sovvagn	*sleeper*
restaurangvagn	______

NEW EXPRESSIONS

sommarlov	*summer break*
hälsa på	*visit*
en påhälsning	______
föreslå	*suggest*
ett förslag	______
kul	*that will be fun*
fortsätta	*continue*
en fortsättning	______
faktiskt	*actually*
skoj	*fun*
det beror på	*that depends*
helt enkelt	*quite simply*
kolla, kontrollera	*check*
en kontrollant	______
trängselskatt	*congestion tax*

Conversation 1

05.02 *A family discusses where they are going this summer.*

1 Where do they want to go and how do they intend to travel?

Pappa	Snart är det sommarlov! Vad tycker ni vi ska göra?
Patrik	Vi vill åka och hälsa på mormor och morfar!
Mamma	Vi kan åka dit med buss nästa vecka, och sedan fortsätta därifrån till faster Eva och farbror Hans.
Sara	Ja, hurra, då får vi träffa våra kusiner! Hur åker vi dit?
Pappa	Det är ju lite längre, så då tycker jag vi tar tåget, det är snabbare.
Patrik	Kan vi ta det riktigt snabba, X2000?
Pappa	Ja, jag ska kolla tidtabellen så får vi se. Om vi tar tåget dit så kan vi ju faktiskt flyga hela vägen tillbaka.
Sara	Både buss och tåg och flygplan, skoj!
Mamma	Kanske kan vi hyra en bil i stället och köra hela vägen, om det inte kostar för mycket?
Pappa	Ja, vi hör med en biluthyrare vad de har för priser.
Mamma	Det gör vi. Vi planerar vidare när vi har kontaktat en resebyrå, som kollar upp de andra alternativen!

2 Find the Swedish for the following phrases:

- **a** We'll take the train.
- **b** It's faster.
- **c** We can rent a car instead.
- **d** The travel agency checks the other options.

3 Read this summary of the dialogue, then answer the questions.

Det är snart sommarlov. Pappa. Mamma, Sara och Patrik diskuterar vad de ska göra. De ska åka buss till mormor och morfar. De tar tåget till faster Eva, farbror Hans och kusinerna. Sedan ska de flyga tillbaka hem.

- **a** What are the children called?
- **b** How are they travelling to their grandparents?
- **c** How are they going to their cousins?
- **d** How will they return home?

Language discovery

1 HOW TO USE THE CORRECT FORM OF ADJECTIVES

Adjectives agree with their nouns in gender (non-neuter and neuter), number (singular and plural) and indefinite/definite form. For neuter words, **-t** is added to the basic form of the adjective, and for plural words **-a** is added. In the definite form (after **den**, **det**, **de**) the adjective always takes an **-a** (except when referring to male nouns, see language tip).

en hög byggnad (*a high building*)**, ett högt hus**

två höga byggnader, två höga hus

den höga byggnaden, de höga byggnaderna

det höga huset, de höga husen

2 COMPARATIVE AND SUPERLATIVE FORMS OF ADJECTIVES

Adjectives can be used to compare things (this one is better than that one). This is called the comparative (ending in either **-are** or **-re**).

They can also be used to say that something is *the best*, *longest*, *worst*, *prettiest* and so on. This is called the superlative (ending in either **-ast** or **-st**):

Snabb, snabbare, snabbast

Hög, högre, högst

Some also change the vowel:

Låg, lägre, lägst (*low*)

Lång, längre, längst

Stor, större, störst

Ung, yngre, yngst (*young*)

A few adjectives are compared irregularly, among them:

Gammal, äldre, äldst (*old*)

God, bra, bättre, bäst (*good*)

Dålig, sämre, sämst (*bad*)

Liten, mindre, minst

> Adjectives referring to male nouns take an **-e** in the definite form:
> **Den gamle mannen**, but **den gamla kvinnan**

3 TELLING THE TIME

The answer to the question **Vad är klockan?** or **Hur mycket är klockan?** (*What time is it?*) is either **den är**, **klockan är** or **hon är** (*it is*).

The 30 minutes after the full hour are **över**, the following 30 are **i**. Thus, between five and six o'clock, these are the five-minute intervals: **Klockan är fem**, **fem över fem**, **tio över fem**, **kvart över fem**, **tjugo över fem**. *Twenty-five minutes past five* is **fem i halv sex**, an exception to the rule. *Half past five* is **halv sex**. *Twenty-five minutes to six* is **fem över halv sex**, also an exception, then **tjugo i sex**, **kvart i sex**, **tio i sex**, **fem i sex**, **klockan är sex**. Note that *half past five* is **halv sex**, *half past six* **halv sju**, etc. The equivalent of *a.m.* is **fm** (**förmiddag**) and *p.m.* is **em** (**eftermiddag**), but the 24-hour clock is used in timetables: midnight is 00.00, noon is 12.00, 1 a.m. is 01.00, 1 p.m. is 13.00, 11 a.m. is 11.00 and 11 p.m. is 23.00.

4 DIRECTIONS

The cardinal points of the compass are **norr**, **söder**, **väster** and **öster**. Going in these directions is expressed by adding **-ut**: **norrut**, **söderut**, **västerut**, **österut** (coming from them is expressed by adding **-ifrån**: **norrifrån** (= **från norr**), **söderifrån**, **västerifrån**, **österifrån**).

Malmö ligger i söder, Umeå i norr, Stockholm i öster och Göteborg i väster. När jag flyger från Malmö till Stockholm reser jag norrut. När jag tar tåget från Stockholm till Göteborg reser jag västerut.

Practice

1 Translate into Swedish

- **a** My youngest sister is seven years younger than me.
- **b** Mount Everest is the highest mountain.
- **c** The train to Stockholm is faster than the car.
- **d** To bike is slower but better.
- **e** She flies north and he drives south.
- **f** Gothenburg is in the west, Kalmar in the east.

2 Match the Swedish and the English.

a	Fem över halv åtta på kvällen	**1**	8.30 a.m.
b	Halv två på natten	**2**	11.59 p.m.
c	Halv nio på morgonen	**3**	Noon
d	Fem i halv tio på kvällen	**4**	1.30 a.m.

e	Klockan tolv mitt på dagen	**5**	9.25 p.m.
f	En minut i midnatt	**6**	7.35 p.m.

3 Fill in the missing words.

a Hon är en ______ (*young*) flicka.

b Han är ett ______ (*big*) barn.

c Hon har några ______ (*Swedish*) sillburkar.

VOCABULARY

05.03

sill *herring*

burk *tin, jar*

fönster *window*

gång *aisle*

Conversation 2

05.04 *Agneta is at Sturup, the airport outside Malmö. She runs into her friend Ulla who is leaving for Arlanda on the same plane.*

1 Where are they going?

Agneta Hej Ulla, vart är du på väg?

Ulla Jag ska upp till Stockholm och vidare till min dotter i Boston.

Agneta Så spännande! Jag ska bara flyga upp till min son som fyller trettio i morgon.

Ulla Hur firar ni hans födelsedag?

Agneta Vi tar färjan till Djurgården, ser på Skansen och äter lunch där.

Ulla Du, vi måste gå till gaten!

Agneta Men oj, var har jag lagt mitt boarding-kort?

They go to the gate while Agneta rummages through her handbag...

Agneta Usch, jag blir alltid så nervös när jag är ute och reser!

Ulla Ja, alltid mycket att tänka på. Pass, pengar, biljett, kreditkort...

Agneta Vad tar du med till din dotter i Amerika?

Ulla Kalles kaviar, svenskt kaffe, några sillburkar.

Agneta Sådär, nu är vi på planet. Jag sitter vid gången och du har fönsterplats.

2 Read the conversation once more, then answer these questions:

a Why is Ulla going to Boston?
b What is Agneta planning to do in Stockholm?
c What is Ulla bringing her daughter?

Speaking

05.05 **Play the part of Ulla in this conversation.**

Agneta	Hej Ulla, vart ska du resa?
Ulla	*I am flying to my daughter in Boston.*
Agneta	Vad tar du med dig till henne?
Ulla	*Caviar, some herring and Swedish coffee, much stronger than American coffee.*
Agneta	Det är pingstafton i morgon, då fyller min son trettio år.
Ulla	*My daughter is younger, she's 25. How do you celebrate his birthday?*

Reading

Look at the timetable on the opposite page and figure out the following:

a You can take two direct trains from Stockholm to Abisko. When do they leave, and when do they arrive?
b If you take a morning train, you have to change in Umeå. How many minutes do you have between the trains there?
c If you want to continue from Abisko to the northern border of Sweden (Riksgränsen), how long time does the journey take?
d The train for Narvik on the Norwegian coast leaves Abisko at 16.31. When does it arrive in Narvik?
e If Anna and Sven want to travel from Malmö to Abisko without breaking their journey in Stockholm, how many hours and minutes will it take?

40 Malmö-Stockholm-Umeå-Boden-Narvik			
fr Malmö C		12.11	16.11
fr Stockholm C	10.22	17.58	22.12
t Umeå C	18.22	01.51	06.45
fr Umeå C	18.43	01.56	06.50
t Boden C	22.18	05.36	10.30
fr Boden C		06.05	10.50
t Abisko turiststation		11.40	16.31
t Riksgränsen		12.34	17.19
t Narvik		13.24	18.12

Writing

Ulla would like to send a postcard from Boston to her mother in Stockholm. Write it for her, in Swedish.

These are some nouns you may want to use: **sol** (*sun*), **väder** (*weather*), **vatten**, **segelbåtar** (*sailing boats*), **bilar**, **turister**, **restauranger**, **kaféer**, **nattliv** (*night life*), **jazzfestival**, **hummer** (*lobster*), **konstgalleri** (*art gallery*). **Sol**, **båt**, **bil**, **turist**, **restaurang**, **festival**, **hummer** are non-neuter words, the rest neuter.

These are some adjectives: **liten**, **stor**, **billig**, **dyr**, **ung**, **gammal**, **ful** (*ugly*), **vacker** (*beautiful*).

And these are some verbs: **segla**, **bada**, **lyssna på musik**, **äta**, **koppla av**.

Test yourself

1 Give these times in Swedish:

a 6 a.m.

b 9.25 a.m.

c 12 noon

d 1.45 p.m.

e 4.30 p.m.

f 11.35 p.m.

2 Fill in the missing Swedish words.

a I England kör man på vänster sida, men sedan 1967 har Sverige ________.

b Stockholm ligger ________ om Malmö och ________ om Göteborg.

c I Stockholm kan man ta bussen, men också ________.

3 Translate the following into Swedish:

a The train is faster than (**än**) the bus.

b It is further (= longer) to aunt Eva and Uncle Hans than to grandmother and grandfather.

c We'll check how much a hire car costs.

d The old man is older than the old woman.

SELF CHECK

	I CAN...
○	... plan a journey and order tickets.
○	... tell the time.
○	... use the points of the compass.
○	... use the positive, comparative and superlative forms of adjectives.

6 Att hitta rätt

Finding your way

In this unit you will learn how to:

- ***ask for and follow directions.***
- ***recognize some basic traffic signs.***
- ***use ordinal numbers.***
- ***use the imperative form of verbs.***

CEFR: (A1) *Can understand everyday signs and notices.* **(A2)** *Can ask for and give directions.*

Stockholm

Central Stockholm is easily covered by foot. Sergels Torg is named after the 18th century sculptor Tobias Sergel whose workshop was here until it was destroyed in the brutal city 'renewal' of the 1960s. On opposite sides of Hamngatan (in spite of its name not very close to a harbour) are the department store NK, short for Nordiska Kompaniet, and the nearby shopping centre Gallerian. Kungsträdgården is a green oasis in summer with an ice rink for skating in winter. On one side of Strandvägen are stately late-19th century apartment buildings, on the other there is water, part of Östersjön (*the Baltic*). Djurgården, once a royal pasture (**djur** means *animal*), has interesting museums like the ethnographic Nordiska museet and the art museums Liljevalchs and Waldemarsudde. Vasamuseet houses the splendid but ill-fated 17th century warship Vasa. Skansen is an open-air museum with a mini zoo. Gröna Lund nearby is an amusement park.

Getting around

Gata (*street*) is used in urban areas as is **väg** (*road*), but **väg** is also a road leading to or from nearby cities, for example Malmövägen in Ystad and Ystadvägen in Malmö. **Gränd** (*alley*) is short and narrow, **återvändsgränd** is a *cul-de-sac*. An **allé** is often lined by trees. **Aveny** is less common, though **Kungsportsavenyn** or simply **Avenyn** is the central street in Gothenburg. That Sweden is a monarchy is obvious in the naming of streets in most cities.

Give the English names for the following streets.

Kungsgatan, Drottninggatan, Hamngatan, Nygatan, Storgatan, Kyrkogatan, Klostergatan, Skolgatan, Villavägen

Vocabulary builder

06.01 **Look at the words and complete the missing English expressions. Then listen and try to imitate the pronunciation of the speakers.**

DIRECTIONS

ta till höger	*turn right*
ta till vänster	*turn left*
rakt fram	*straight ahead*
tvärs över	*across*
korsa gatan	*cross the street*
gå över	*go across*
vandra vidare	*walk on*
stanna till	*stop at*
stan (staden)	*the town, the city*
bibliotek	*library*
svänga in	*turn into*
trafikljus	________
kvarter	*block*
rondell	*roundabout*
gård, innergård	*courtyard of an apartment block*
parkera	________
parkeringsplats	________

DRIVING

öva, övning	*train, training*
körkort	*driving licence*
säkerhetsbälte	*seatbelt*
visa tecken	*indicate*
förbjuden	*forbidden, not allowed*
tanka bilen	________
bensinstation	________
fotgängare	*pedestrian*

Conversation 1

06.02 *Two tourists arrive in Stockholm and want to visit Skansen, the open-air museum. Follow their progress on the map of Stockholm.*

1 Who do they ask for directions?

Turisterna	Ursäkta, hur kommer vi till Skansen härifrån?
Polisen	Gå vidare till Sergels Torg och fråga igen där.
Turisterna	Är det bara rakt fram?
Polisen	Ja, gå över Vasagatan här vid övergångsstället och vandra vidare längs Klarabergsgatan till Sergels Torg.
Turisterna	Tack, det klarar vi nog.

En kvart senare, på Sergels Torg:

Turisterna	Vi frågar damen därborta. Förlåt, hur hittar vi fram till Skansen härifrån?
Damen	Gå längs Hamngatan. NK ligger på vänster hand, där kan ni titta in, och Kungsträdgården ser ni på höger hand.
Turisterna	Där tror jag vi stannar till och tar en kaffe-paus!
Damen	Det är en bra idé. Fortsätt sedan rakt fram till Strandvägen. Följ vattnet ända fram till bron på höger sida och gå över den.
Turisterna	Var är vi då?
Damen	Då är ni på Djurgården med alla museer. Nordiska museet är det första och Vasamuseet med Vasaskeppet det andra.
Turisterna	Hur långt är det sedan kvar till Skansen som väl är det tredje?
Damen	Tja, kanske tio minuter. När ni sett Vasamuseet är ni strax framme.
Turisterna	Tack så mycket! Nu vandrar vi vidare!

2 Read the conversation again and answer the following questions.

a Can they do some shopping on the way?
b Why do they take a break at Kungsträdgården?
c Which museums can they visit on Djurgården?
d What can be seen in Vasamuseet?

3 Match the Swedish to the English.

a det andra	**1** first
b det tredje	**2** second
c det första	**3** third

4 Translate the following into Swedish, using imperative verbs.

a Cross Vasagatan.
b Continue along Klarabergsgatan.
c Walk along Hamngatan.

Language discovery

1 ORDINAL NUMBERS, FROM THE FIRST TO THE MILLIONTH

06.03 **Learn these ordinals by heart (utantill) as you go along.**

första, andra, tredje, fjärde, femte, sjätte, sjunde, åttonde, nionde, tionde, elfte, tolfte, trettonde, fjortonde, femtonde, sextonde, sjuttonde, artonde, nittonde, tjugonde, tjugoförsta, and so on.

trettionde, **fyrtionde**, **femtionde**, **sextionde**, **sjuttionde**, **åttionde**, **nittionde**

hundrade, **tusende**, **miljonte**

Examples: **Affären är på femte avenyn** (*The shop is on Fifth Avenue*). **Det är sjunde gången jag är i Stockholm** (*I am in Stockholm for the seventh time*). **Jag tar hissen till artonde våningen** (*I take the lift to the 18th floor*). **Det är tusende gången jag säger till dig att inte köra för fort** (*I have told you a thousand times not to drive too fast*).

2 IMPERATIVE FORM OF VERBS

The imperative forms of verbs express wishes, orders or commands, and are the same as the verb stem:

Hjälp!	*Help!*
Se upp!	*Look out!*
Kom hit!	*Come here!*
Gå bort!	*Go away!*
Försvinn!	*Disappear! Make yourself scarce!*
Håll tyst!	*Keep quiet!*

There are more polite ways of expressing the same order or command: **Kan du komma hit? Var snäll och kom hit! Var vänlig håll tyst!**

3 PHRASAL VERBS

In set verb expressions, an unstressed verb is often followed by a stressed preposition or adverb:

hälsa på (*visit*), **komma dit** (*get there*), **svänga in** (*turn into*), **köra förbi** (*drive past*), **sätta på** (*turn on*), **hitta fram** (*find one's way*)

Note that depending on the stress **Jag hälsar på honom** has two meanings: *I greet him* (if the verb is stressed) or *I visit him* (if the preposition is stressed).

Practice

1 Change the following cardinal numbers into ordinals. The first has been done for you as an example.

a Jag bor på våning sexton – jag bor på sextonde våningen.
b Jag svänger in på gata nummer sex härifrån.
c Eva bor i hus nummer tre härifrån.
d 14/3 är fjortonde i tredje (den fjortonde dagen i den tredje månaden). Vad är 13/4?
e Stilleståndsdagen (*Armistice Day*) den 11/11 är...

2 **Turn the following questions and statements into orders by using a verb in the imperative.**

a Kan du tala om hur vi kommer till Skansen?
b Sedan fortsätter ni rakt fram till Strandvägen.
c Ni går härifrån till Sergels Torg.
d Frågar du damen där borta om resten av vägen?
e Nu vandrar vi vidare till Vasamuséet.

3 **Translate the verbs in the following sentences, showing that you understand which of them are phrasal verbs.**

a Jag kör på gatan.
b Kör inte på bilen där borta.
c Vi hälsar på hos moster Emma (= *at her place*) varje dag.
d Vi säger hej eller god dag när vi hälsar på någon.

In order to get a Swedish **körkort** (*driving licence*) you need to be at least 18 years old. You also have to take a **syntest** to prove that you have good vision. Then you either enrol at **körskola** or **trafikskola** (*traffic school*), or start training privately (**körträna privat**). You will have to pass a **teoriprov** (*theory test*) before being examined on your **uppkörningsprov** (*driving skills*). Half a day is set aside for a mandatory introduction to different risk factors like **droger**, **alkohol**, **trötthet** (*drugs, alcohol, tiredness*) and you also have to drive for a certain distance on ice (**halkkörning**), giving you an idea how to handle slippery conditions. All this takes time and money but should result in careful and cautious drivers. The drink driving limit (**0.2 promille**) is close to zero tolerance, with obvious benefits as can be seen in the **trafikstatistik** (*traffic statistics*). All cars must have a **bilförsäkring** (*be insured*).

Speaking

06.04 **Listen to the conversation once more, then play the part of the policeman.**

Turisterna	Hur kommer vi till Skansen härifrån?
Policeman	*You had better walk from here to Sergels Torg.*
Turisterna	Är det bara rakt fram?
Policeman	*Yes, cut across Vasagatan and continue along Klarabergsgatan.*
Turisterna	Tack, det klarar vi nog.
Policeman	*Good luck, have a nice day.*

Det är bäst att du går rakt fram = *You had better walk straight on*: Note that the verb tense differs in Swedish and English.

Pronunciation

Answer the following questions in Swedish, using ordinal numbers.

- **a** Midsommardagen 2013 var den tjugoandra i sjätte. När var det midsommarafton?
- **b** Juldagen är den tjugofemte i tolfte. När är det julafton?
- **c** Nyårsdagen är den första i första. När är det nyårsafton?
- **d** Jag fyller år den trettonde i fjärde. När fyller du år?

VOCABULARY

06.05

centralen (centralstationen)	*central railway station*
övergångsställe	*pedestrian crossing*
klara	*manage*
förlåt, ursäkta	*excuse me, pardon*
glass	*ice cream*
glas	*glass*
bro	*bridge*

Conversation 2

06.06 *Jenny, who will soon turn 18, wants to get her driver's licence. She practises driving with her mother.*

1 Which imperatives are used in this conversation?

Mamma	Ta på dig säkerhetsbältet innan vi startar och kör rakt fram till rondellen.
Jenny	Och så svänger jag till vänster?
Mamma	Bra. Men kör inte för fort. Sakta ner!
Jenny	Ja, jag vill ju inte ha fortkörningsböter!
Mamma	Stanna vid stoppskylten, visa tecken, vi ska köra till höger.
Jenny	Kan vi inte stanna snart och köpa glass?
Mamma	Jo, men just här är det parkering förbjuden.
Jenny	Men här då? Det står 60 minuter på skylten!
Mamma	Det går bra. Sedan måste vi tanka bilen.

Jenny	Jag kör in på bensinstationen. Ska vi ha full tank?
Mamma	Ja, fyll tanken. Bra. Kör vidare.
Jenny	Typiskt, det blev rött ljus.
Mamma	Låt fotgängarna gå över, här är ett övergångsställe.
Jenny	Pust, nu är vi framme. Det var jobbigt.
Mamma	Ja, men du kör riktigt bra. Snart fyller du ju 18 år och kan köra upp och få ditt körkort.

2 Find the expressions in the conversation that mean the following:

a Stop and indicate.
b I don't want any speeding fines.
c Don't drive too fast, take it easy.

Reading

1 Match the English description of the following twelve traffic signs with the Swedish ones.

1 Varning för halka	**a** No entry
2 Vägarbete	**b** No overtaking
3 Älgvarning	**c** No biking
4 Motorväg upphör	**d** Slippery road
5 Övergångsställe	**e** Strong sidewind
6 Se upp för skidåkare	**f** Elk hazard
7 Cykling förbjuden	**g** Road works
8 Stark sidvind	**h** Road narrows
9 Avsmalnande väg	**i** Speed bumps
10 Omkörning förbjuden	**j** End of motorway
11 Infart förbjuden	**k** Pedestrian crossing
12 Varning för farthinder	**l** Beware of skier

2 Now match the twelve signs A–L with their Swedish description 1–12.

Test yourself

1 Fill in the missing words.

a Gå over Vasagatan vid _______ (*the pedestrian crossing*) och vandra vidare _______ (*along*) Klarabergsgatan.

b Där _______ (*think*) jag vi stannar och tar _______ (*a coffee break*).

c Följ _______ (*the water*) ända fram till _______ (*the bridge*).

d Tag på dig _______ (*the seat belt*) innan vi startar och kör inte för _______ (*fast*).

2 Translate into Swedish.

a Which direction do I take at the roundabout?

b We are on the third floor.

c Continue straight ahead, you'll soon be there.

d You drive quite well.

SELF CHECK

	I CAN...
○	... ask for directions in a city.
○	... recognize Swedish traffic signs.
○	... use imperative forms of verbs.
○	... change cardinal numbers into ordinals.

R2 Review 2

1 Fill in the nouns that are missing in the following text.

Det finns många populära ______ (*cafés*) i Gamla Stan dit ______ (*Stockholmers*) som jag går. Jag dricker två ______ (*cups*) kaffe, och jag läser ______ (*books*) och ______ (*newspapers*) på tre ______ (*languages*). Ibland sitter ______ (*musicians*) på några av ______ (*the chairs*) och spelar till mitt morgonkaffe.

2 Translate these sentences into Swedish.

- **a** Lennart is the youngest of the brothers; his brothers are much older.
- **b** Kebnekaise is the highest mountain in Sweden, but much lower than Mont Blanc.
- **c** Gothenburg is smaller than Stockholm but bigger than Malmö.
- **d** In October the weather is worse than in July but better than in February.

3 Write the following times of the day in words and in Swedish, adding the words for *morning*, *afternoon* and *evening*, like this: 8.35 a.m. = fem över halv nio på morgonen.

- **a** 7.30 a.m.
- **b** 11.20 a.m.
- **c** 3.15 p.m.
- **d** 11.25 p.m.

4 Turn these sentences into orders, using the imperative form of the verbs.

- **a** Kan du skriva ditt namn här?
- **b** Du måste se upp när det kommer en bil.
- **c** Du svänger till höger i rondellen.
- **d** Kan du trycka din kod i uttagsautomaten?

5 How does the difference in stress affect the meaning in a) and b), and in c) and d)?

- **a** Jag kör på gatan.
- **b** Jag kör på trädet.
- **c** Jag hälsar på honom när jag ser honom på gatan.
- **d** Jag hälsar på min moster i Lund när jag är i Sverige.

6 Write the questions to these answers, using a) när, b) var, c) hur and d) varför.

a August Strindberg föddes 1849, och han dog 1912.

b Han bodde i många städer, både Stockholm, Paris och Berlin.

c Han skrev sina manuskript för hand på gult papper.

d Han träffade sina vänner i Lund den 22 januari 1899 för att fira sin femtioårsdag.

7 Translate the dates into Swedish, using ordinal numbers, like this: *2 March* = **andre mars.**

a 29 February

b 14 July

c 30 November

d 13 December

8 Fill in the missing words.

a När man kör från Stockholm till Malmö kör man ______ (*south*).

b En göteborgare som ska till Stockholm tar tåget ______ (*east*).

c För att komma från Stockholm till Abisko måste man resa ______ (*north*).

d Tåget från Malmö till Köpenhamn går ______ (*west*) över Öresundsbron.

9 Read the text, then answer the questions.

Greta och Barbro är svägerskor. Nu är de ute och handlar tillsammans. De ska köpa presenter till sina barnbarn. Greta köper ett stort pussel till dotterdöttrarna Jytte och Jenny. Barbro köper två böcker till sina dottersöner Per och Mats. Sedan dricker de en kopp kaffe på ett kafé och tar bussen hem igen.

a How are Greta and Barbro related?

b What are they out shopping for?

c What does Greta buy, and for whom?

d What does Barbro buy, and for whom?

e Where do they relax after shopping?

f How do they get back home?

10 Translate the following sentences into Swedish, showing that you understand nouns and adjectives.

a The popular shop assistant speaks several languages: English, German, French and Spanish.

b He tries on the biggest brown shoes in the shop.

c She likes the red hats, the black dresses and the young men.

d They get money out of the cash machine and fly to China.

e We buy yellow apples, white candles and a red wooden horse from Dalecarlia.

7 Svenska matvanor

Food customs in Sweden

In this unit you will learn how to:

- ***order at a restaurant.***
- ***write a shopping list.***
- ***follow a recipe.***
- ***use the past tense of verbs.***

CEFR: (A2) *Can order a meal. Can follow short, simple written directions.*

Eating in Sweden

Husmanskost is simple but nourishing food based on seasonal and local ingredients like **potatis** (*potatoes*), **kål** (*cabbage*), **morötter** (*carrots*), **rovor** (*turnips*), **lök** (*onions*), **äpplen** (*apples*), **lingon** (*lingonberries*), **blåbär** (*blueberries*), **svamp** (*mushrooms*), **vete**, **råg**, **korn** and **havre** (*wheat, rye, barley* and *oats*), **mejeriprodukter** (*dairy products*) like **mjölk** (*milk*), **grädde** (*cream*), **smör** (*butter*), **ost** (*cheese*) and **filmjölk** (*natural yogurt*) plus **ägg** (*eggs*), **fisk** and **fläsk** (*pork*), and more sparingly **lamm** (*lamb*) and **nötkött** (*beef*). Traditional dishes are **potatismos** and **rotmos** (*mashed potatoes, mashed turnips*), **sill** (*fried or pickled herring*) **och potatis**, **äpplepaj**, **havregrynsgröt** (*porridge*), **äggakaka** (*omelette with bacon*), **köttbullar med lingon**, **pytti-i-panna** (similar to *bubble and squeak*), **kalops** (*beef stew*) **med inlagda rödbetor** (*pickled beetroot*). **Ärtsoppa** (*pea soup*) **och pannkakor** is the staple Thursday diet. **Persilja** (parsley) and **dill** are the most commonly used herbs.

While staying in a Swiss guesthouse in June 1886, the Swedish writer August Strindberg (1849–1912) wrote a letter to a friend about the ample breakfast he was served:

'För 3 fr 50 har jag hel pension. Min frukost är furstlig (princely). Kaffe, mjölk, skorpor (rusks), bröd, smör, ost, honung, sylt, ägg så många jag vill äta. Det är Schlaraffenland.'

What did he get on his breakfast menu for 3 francs 50 centimes (including board)?

Vocabulary builder

07.01 **Look at the words and complete the missing English expressions. Then listen and try to imitate the pronunciation of the speakers.**

IN A RESTAURANT

fönsterbord	*table by the window*
matsedel	*menu*
avsluta	*finish*
bricka	*tray*
bestick	*cutlery*
gaffel	*fork*
sked	*spoon*
kniv	________
käka	*to eat*
disk	*counter*
Får jag be om matsedeln?	*Can I have the menu, please?*
Kan jag få betala, tack?	*Can I have the bill, please?*
Hovmästaren!	*Waiter!*

MENU ITEMS

rödspätta	*flounder, sole*
oxfilé	*fillet steak*
lax	*salmon*
fiskrätt	*fish course*
kötträtt	*meat course*
förrätt	*starter*
huvudrätt	________
efterrätt	*dessert*
lättstekt	*rare*
välstekt	________

NEW EXPRESSIONS

älsklingsblomma	*favourite flower*
knallrött	*bright red*
tulpan	*tulip*

Conversation 1

07.02 *Ebba is invited to a restaurant by Sven on her birthday. He has already booked a table by the window, and has bought her flowers.*

1 What do they choose from the menu?

Kyparen	Välkomna, här är fönsterbordet som ni bokade. Jag kommer strax med matsedeln.
Ebba	Så trevligt här är. Nu ska vi se vad som finns på menyn idag.
Kyparen	Vi har också dagens special, som är rödspätta som fiskrätt och oxfilé som kötträtt.
Ebba	Jag tar gärna en räkcocktail som förrätt.
Sven	Och jag tar en gravad lax-toast.
Ebba	Huvudrätt…nu ska vi se. Gärna en fiskrätt. Varför inte dagens special, rödspättan?
Sven	Låter bra. Men jag tror jag vill ha en kötträtt. Oxfilé, det tar jag.
Kyparen	Ska det vara lättstekt, medium eller välstekt?
Sven	Välstekt, tack. Ebba, vad tar vi till efterrätt?
Ebba	En chokladmousse för mig, tack.
Sven:	Ja, det tror jag blir bra för mig med. Och sedan avslutar vi med varsin kopp kaffe.
Kyparen	Varsågoda, här kommer förrätterna. Smaklig måltid!
Sven	Grattis på födelsedagen, Ebba! Skål!
Ebba	Tack Sven, och tack för de knallröda tulpanerna som är mina älsklingsblommor nu på våren.

2 Read the conversaton again and answer the following questions.

a What table did Sven book?

b How does he want his meat cooked?

c Which kind of flowers and what colour has he bought for Ebba?

d What time of the year is it?

Language discovery

Read the conversation again. Find the phrase that means *Here is the table by the window that you booked***.**

1 PAST TENSE OF VERBS

a) Most verbs are regular, ending in **-de** or **-dde** in the past tense: **boka** (*to book*) becomes **bokade**; **tro** (*to believe*) becomes **trodde**.

b) Verbs whose stems end in **k**, **p**, **s** and **t** (all unvoiced consonants) take **-te** in the past tense: **åka** (*to travel*) becomes **åkte**, **köpa** (*to buy*) becomes **köpte**, **läsa** (*to read*) becomes **läste**, **möta** (*to meet*) becomes **mötte**.

c) Some verbs are irregular and change their vowels in the past tense: **finna** (*to find*) becomes **fann**; **vrida** (*to turn*) becomes **vred**; **bjuda** (*to bid, invite*) becomes **bjöd**; **ta** (*to take*) becomes **tog**; **sätta** (*to put*) becomes **satte**; **gå** (*to go*) becomes **gick**; **se** (*to see*) becomes **såg**; **le** (*to smile*) becomes **log**; **ligga** (*to lie*) becomes **låg**; **ge** (*to give*) becomes **gav**; **dö** (*to die*) becomes **dog**; **låta** (*to sound*) becomes **lät**.

2 PRONOUNS

The pronoun **som** corresponds to *who*, *that* or *which*.

Ebba, som fyller år, får blommorna på bordet.

Ebba, who has her birthday, gets the flowers on the table.

Blommorna, som står på bordet, är till Ebba.

The flowers that are on the table are for Ebba.

Bordet, som är dukat, har blommor till Ebba.

The table which is laid has flowers for Ebba.

Ebba som jag gav blommorna till...

Ebba, to whom I gave the flowers... (Note that the preposition till has to be placed at the very end.)

Practice

1 Change these verbs from present to past tense.

Regular verbs:

Bokar, önskar, börjar, har, funderar, verkar, tror, avslutar

Irregular verbs:

Kommer, kan, blir, får, finns, tar, är, låter, vill, föreslår

2 In the following passage, look for the same verbs in the past tense and translate the sentences into English.

Jag kom till Göteborg i går. Hon kunde inte komma. Ebba blev glad när hon fick blommorna. Lax fanns inte på menyn. Hon tog fisk och han tog kött. Musiken var för hög (*too loud*), det lät förskräckligt (*horrible*). Han ville ha oxfilé, och hon rödspätta. Ebba föreslog chokladmousse.

3 Translate the following sentences into Swedish.

- **a** The girl who sits at (**vid**) the table is my sister.
- **b** The food that we eat is very nice.
- **c** The three friends who have lunch at IKEA are colleagues.

Speaking

07.03 **Listen to the conversation once more, then play the part of the waiter.**

Ebba	Nu ska vi se vad som finns på matsedeln.
Waiter	*Today's special is sole and fillet steak.*
Sven	Jag tror jag vill ha en kötträtt.
Waiter	*Would you like it rare, medium or well done?*
Sven	Välstekt. tack. Och sedan chokladmousse för oss båda.
Waiter	*And you will round off with a cup of coffee?*

IKEA

Ingvar Kamprad, an entrepreneur from Småland, one of the provinces in southern Sweden, started his own company in 1943. He was 17 at the time, and he chose for its name his own initials plus those of the farm he grew up on (Emtaryd), and the nearest village (Agunnaryd); IKEA was born. Based on mail order collapsible furniture for self-assembly, it soon proved extremely successful. The firm has grown into a huge worldwide enterprise with over 350 stores in 40 countries. The largest store is still the one at Kungens Kurva in south Stockholm, established in 1965 and with an area of 55,000 square metres. Other more recent ones in China and Germany are almost as big. All Swedish IKEA stores and most of those abroad have their own restaurants. Swedes abroad find them an ideal meeting place, and the food stores within them carry a wide variety of Swedish food specialities: **inlagd sill**, **köttbullar**, **lingonsylt**, **kaviar**, **knäckebröd** (*crispbread*) and much more.

VOCABULARY

07.04

satsa	*bet on, go for*
lova	*promise*
mätt	*full*
ingå	*included*
hålla sig till	*keep to*
kanelbulle	*cinnamon bun*
mandelkaka	*almond cake*

Conversation 2

07.05 *Per and his friends Sanna and David usually go to IKEA during their lunch break for a quick meal.*

1 Describe what they choose.

Per	Jag satsar på köttbullarna som vanligt. Jag gillar svensk husmanskost.
David	Jag tar laxen idag.
Sanna	Jag tar soppa. Niklas har lovat laga middag idag så jag får inte vara för mätt.

De tar varsin bricka, bestick, glas, och vandrar längs disken, där maten serveras.

Per	Köttbullar, tack, brun sås, fyra potatisar och mycket lingonsylt.

David	Kan jag få laxen, tack, och bara tre potatisar.
Sanna	Jag tar soppan själv där borta. Det är torsdag, ju, så det är ärtsoppa idag, och bröd och dricka ingår.
Per	Jag tror jag håller mig till vatten.
David	Det gör jag med.
Sanna	Men kaffe på maten ska vi väl ha allihop? Jag ska ha en kanelbulle, men ni tar väl mandelkaka, som vanligt?
Per & David	Självklart! Sådär, det ska bli gott! Nu käkar vi!
Sanna	Börja ni, jag tog fel bestick! Man kan ju inte äta soppa med kniv och gaffel! Jag måste hämta en sked!

2 Read the conversation again and answer the following questions.

a Why does Sanna go for a less substantial meal?

b What is included in her choice?

c Why couldn't she do with just a knife and fork?

NEW EXPRESSIONS

07.06

deciliter (dl)	*1/10 of a litre*
tesked (tsk)	*teaspoon*
mjöl	*flour*
mjölk	*milk*
vispa	*whip*
vispgrädde	*whipped cream*
steka	*fry*
smälta	*melt*
smet	*batter*
sylt	*jam*
hallon	*raspberries*
jordgubbar	*strawberries*

Reading

Here is the recipe for Swedish thin pancakes.

Recept på tunna pannkakor:

Ingredienser:

2,5 dl vetemjöl

5 dl mjölk

3 ägg

½ tsk salt

1 tsk socker

50 gram smör

Gör så här:

Vispa samman mjöl, mjölk och ägg. Smält smöret i en stekpanna. Häll det smälta smöret i smeten. Häll lagom mycket smet i stekpannan, stek på ena sidan, vänd sedan och stek på den andra sidan. Fortsätt tills smeten är slut. Då har du fått cirka femton pannkakor. Servera med lingonsylt, hallonsylt eller jordgubbssylt och gärna vispgrädde. Mums!

Read the recipe again and answer the following questions.

- **a** Which are the three main ingredients in pancakes?
- **b** What does **vändstekt** mean?
- **c** What extras would a typical Swedish family have with their pancakes?
- **d** Why is there no need for butter in the frying pan?

Listening

07.07 *The mother in the family drives down to the supermarket to do her weekly shopping. Listen, then use it for the writing exercise that follows.*

Det är lördag och mamma tar bilen och åker till affären för att veckohandla.

Hon har en LÅNG inköpslista (*shopping list*). Så här ser den ut:

Bröd, både limpa (*loaf*) och knäckebröd

Flingor (*cornflakes*), müsli

Mjölk, filmjölk, joghurt, juice

Smör, ost, ägg

Apelsinmarmelad

Korv, köttfärs (*minced meat*)

Potatis, lök, morötter, tomater

Kaffe, the

Pasta eller spaghetti

Ketchup, senap (*mustard*)

Tvättmedel (*washing powder*), diskmedel (*dishwashing liquid*), toalettpapper

Tändstickor, stearinljus

Usch, tänker hon, det här blir dyrt (*expensive*); varför måste allt ta slut samtidigt (*run out all at once*)?

Nu är det klart. Nu ska hon bara be Anders att han går ner till systembolaget och köper några flaskor vin och lite öl (*beer*).

 Writing

Write your own shopping list based on the listening exercise, but this time only write down the items that would be needed on a breakfast table.

Test yourself

1 Change the verbs in these sentences from past to present tense.
  a Ebba fyllde år.
  b Sven bjöd henne på middag ute.
  c Per, David och Sanna gick till IKEA.
  d De åt lunch i restaurangen där.
  e Per gillade husmanskosten.
  f Sanna tog fel bestick.

2 Match the Swedish and the English.

a Matsedel	1 tray
b Förrätt	2 almond cakes
c Smaklig måltid	3 dessert
d Huvudrätt	4 pea soup
e Bestick	5 salmon
f Bricka	6 menu
g Ärtsoppa	7 main course
h Mandelkakor	8 starter
i Efterrätt	9 bon appétit
j Lax	10 cutlery

3 Translate the following sentences into Swedish.
  a The music was too loud, it sounded horrible.
  b Bright red tulips are my favourite flowers.
  c I will go for meatballs. I like basic Swedish food.
  d Pour enough batter into the frying pan, fry the pancake on one side, then turn it over.

SELF CHECK

	I CAN...
○	**... order a meal at a restaurant.**
○	**... write a shopping list.**
○	**... follow instructions.**
○	**... use the past tense.**

8 Hemma

At home

In this unit you will learn how to:

- ***describe your home.***
- ***describe yourself.***
- ***use reflexive pronouns.***
- ***use verbs in different tenses.***

CEFR: (A2) *Can write about everyday aspects of your environment. Can understand short, simple texts containing the highest frequency vocabulary.*

Swedes at home

Swedes spend much of their time **inomhus** (*indoors*), and they make their homes **trivsamma och inbjudande** (*comfortable and inviting*). Houses are **välisolerade** (*well insulated*) and have **centralvärme** (*central heating*). Thanks to **dubbelfönster** (*double glazed windows*) or even **tredubbla fönster** (*triple glazed windows*) they stay warm even on very cold winter days. **Inredningen** (*the interior decoration*) is often in neutral colours: **ljusa väggar**, **mattor**, **och gardiner** (*light walls*, *carpets* and *curtains*) with **lätta möbler** (*light furniture*). **Fönsterbrädor** (*window sills*) are wide enough to hold **krukväxter** (*pot plants*) so you get greenery indoors. Swedes, proud of their homes, like to show **besökare** (*visitors*) how they live. They often take them on **husesyn** (*a guided tour of the house*).

Some of the nouns above (all of them **en**-nouns) form their plurals with the ending **-or**, **-ar** and **-er**: **mattor**, **fönsterbrädor**; **väggar**, **svenskar**; **gardiner**, **möbler**, **krukväxter**. What are their singular forms?

Vocabulary builder

08.01 **Look at the words and complete the missing English equivalents. Then listen and try to imitate the pronunciation of the speakers.**

AT HOME

källare	*basement*
tambur	*hall*
vardagsrum	*living room*
matrum	*dining room*
arbetsrum	*study*
sovrum	*bedroom*
gästrum	________
barnkammare	________
badrum	________
dusch	*shower*
kök	*kitchen*
trädgård	*garden*
bastu	*sauna*
spis	*oven*
diskmaskin	*dishwasher*
mikrovågsugn	________
kyl (=kylskåp)	*fridge*
frys	________
tvättstuga	*laundry*
tvättmaskin	________
torktumlare	*tumble dryer*
inneskor	*slippers*
skrivbord	*writing desk*
bokhylla	*bookcase*
hörna	*corner*
fortfarande	*still*
använda	*make use of*

Bastu is short for **badstuga** (originally a separate little house for washing oneself). Most other languages would call it by its Finnish name **sauna**.

Conversation 1

08.02 *Margareta and Peter are invited to stay at Helena's place. She takes them on a tour of the house.*

1 Which rooms are they shown?

Helena	Hej, välkomna, så trevligt att ha er här!
Margareta	Tack, roligt att vara här! Vi tar av våra blöta skor här i tamburen och byter till inneskor.
Helena	Gästrummet ligger här till vänster, känn er som hemma!
Peter	Så trevligt! Vi ställer in våra väskor där så länge. Där står de bra.
Helena	Här är vardagsrummet med mathörnan där borta, nära köket.
Margareta	Oj så fint! Och så trevligt med det stora fönstret mot trädgården!
Helena	Från mathörnan kommer man ut på en terrass, så på sommaren äter vi oftast ute.
Peter	Ett så fint och modernt kök, spis med grill, diskmaskin, mikrovågsugn, stor kyl och frys.
Helena	Här har vi arbetsrummet med skrivbord, bokhyllor och en tevehörna. Och går vi vidare kommer vi till barnkammaren.
Margareta	Så trivsamt!
Helena	Här är vårt sovrum, med eget badrum. Tvättstugan med tvättmaskin och torktumlare har vi i källaren. Och det bästa till sist … bastun! Vi älskar att bada bastu! Och bredvid finns en dusch.
Peter	Kan vi få använda bastun senare i kväll?
Helena	Så gärna, det är härligt innan man lägger sig! Nu går vi tillbaka till vardagsrummet och pratar lite före middagen! Sätt er i soffan, i den sitter man bekvämast!

2 Answer the following questions.

a How is the kitchen equipped?
b What can you find in the study?
c Where do they usually eat in summertime?
d Which is the best part of the house, according to Helena?

3 Match the Swedish to the English.

a Gästrummet ligger här till vänster	**1** Sit down on the sofa, it's comfortable to sit on.
b Vi ställer in våra väskor där så länge.	**2** The guest room is there to the left.
c Sätt er i soffan. I den sitter man bekvämt.	**3** We'll put the suitcases here for the time being.

4 Find the Swedish for the following.

a Please feel at home.
b It's nice using the sauna before going to bed.

Language discovery

1 REFLEXIVE PRONOUNS

Reflexive pronouns refer to the subject of the sentence.

mig (jag)	**Jag slog mig.**	*I hit myself/I hurt myself.*
dig (du)	**Du får tänka på dig själv.**	*You must think of yourself.*
sig (han)	**Han lugnade ner sig.**	*He calmed down.*
sig (hon)	**Hon kammade sig.**	*She combed her hair (lit. She combed herself).*
sig (den)	**Den (katten) slickade sig.**	*It (the cat) licked itself.*
sig (det)	**Huset klarade sig i jordbävningen.**	*The house survived the earthquake.*
oss (vi)	**Vi erbjuder oss att hjälpa till.**	*We are offering our help.*
er (ni)	**Ni klarar er inte utan pengar.**	*You won't manage without money.*
sig (de)	**De klarar sig bra.**	*They manage well.*

Slå has several different meanings: **jag slår honom i tennis** (*I beat him at tennis*); **jag slog vad** (*I made a bet*); **jag har slagit sönder fönstret** (*I have broken the window*); **jag ska slå ihjäl flugan** (*I will kill the fly*).

2 THE DIFFERENT TENSES OF THE VERB

The tense of a verb tells you when something takes place.

Present	**Vad händer nu?**	*What happens now?*
Past	**Vad hände i går?**	*What happened yesterday?*
Perfect	**Vad har hänt?**	*What has happened?*
Pluperfect	**Vad hade hänt innan jag kom?**	*What had happened before I came?*
Future	**Vad ska hända i morgon?**	*What will happen tomorrow?*

Note that present tense is often used about something in the future: **Det händer i morgon** (*It will happen tomorrow*).

Here are the infinitive and the five tenses for six different verbs.

Infinitive	Present	Past	Perfect	Pluperfect	Future
bada (*to bathe*)	**badar**	**badade**	**har badat**	**hade badat**	**ska bada**
hänga (*to hang*)	**hänger**	**hängde**	**har hängt**	**hade hängt**	**ska hänga**
besöka (*to visit*)	**besöker**	**besökte**	**har besökt**	**hade besökt**	**ska besöka**
gå (*to walk*)	**går**	**gick**	**har gått**	**hade gått**	**ska gå**
äta (*to eat*)	**äter**	**åt**	**har ätit**	**hade ätit**	**ska äta**
se (*to see*)	**ser**	**såg**	**har sett**	**hade sett**	**ska se**

3 VERBS OF PLACE AND DIRECTION, SITTA/SÄTTA, LIGGA/LÄGGA, STÅ/STÄLLA

Some related verbs distinguish between place and direction. One cannot take an object (the first given here), while the other one can (the second given here).

Jag sitter i soffan. (*I sit on the sofa.*)

Jag sätter mig i soffan. (*I sit down on the sofa.*)

Hon ligger i sängen. (*She lies in bed.*)

Hon lägger katten på sängen. (*She puts the cat down on the bed.*)

Lampan står på bordet. (*The lamp is on the table.*)

Jag ställer lampan på bordet. (*I put the lamp on the table.*)

Practice

1 **Translate the following sentences into Swedish using reflexive verbs.**
   - **a** He hurt himself but he calmed down.
   - **b** I saw that she had combed her hair.

2 **Use the correct tense of the verb in these sentences.**
   - **a** We'll have dinner on the terrace.
   - **b** He had seen an elk in the garden.

3 **Use the correct verbs to show place and direction.**
   - **a** The cat lies on the bed.
   - **b** She has put it there.
   - **c** He sat down on the sofa.
   - **d** Now he sits there.

VOCABULARY
08.03

hittat på	been doing
lära känna	getting to know
tidigare	before, earlier
aldrig	never
pröva	try
deckare	detective stories
flytta	move
äntligen	finally, eventually
anpassa sig	adapt, adjust

Conversation 2

08.04 *Bonnie and Mary live in America. Mary has just returned from a trip overseas.*

1 **Which country has Mary visited?**

Bonnie	Hej, Mary! Var har du varit i sommar?
Mary	Jag har varit i Sverige med familjen.
Bonnie	Kul! Vad har ni hittat på där?
Mary	Vi har sett mycket och lärt känna flera svenskar, vi har badat bastu och sedan hoppat direkt i sjön – det var kallt!

Bonnie	Oj, jag har aldrig badat bastu! Har du gjort det tidigare?
Mary	Ja, vi har prövat det inomhus i Sverige förut; många svenskar har egen bastu. Vad har du själv gjort?
Bonnie	Jag har mest varit hemma. Vädret har varit bra så jag har badat ganska ofta. Och jag har haft tid att läsa deckare.
Mary	Då har du ju haft det skönt! Har du hunnit resa något?
Bonnie	Ja, jag har hälsat på min mamma. Hon har ju flyttat till min syster och har anpassat sig bra där.
Mary	Så bra! Hon har ju haft svårt med sitt stora hus alldeles ensam?
Bonnie	Ja, nu har hon äntligen bestämt sig och vi är alla glada.

2 Answer the following questions.

a What has Mary been doing in Sweden?

b What has Bonnie been doing in America?

Speaking

08.05 **Listen to the conversation once more, then play the part of Mary.**

Bonnie	Hej Mary, välkommen tillbaka. Var har du varit i sommar?
Mary	*We've been in Sweden.*
Bonnie	Kul. Vad har ni hittat på där?
Mary	*We've seen much of Sweden and got to know many Swedes. What have you been doing?*
Bonnie	Jag har varit hemma och läst deckare.
Mary	*Have you had time to travel?*
Bonnie	Jag har hälsat på min mamma som flyttat till min syster.
Mary	*How nice that she has made up her mind.*

The words for many professions often end in **-are**:

Arbetare (*worker*), **snickare** (*carpenter*), **målare** (*painter*), **lärare** (*teacher*), **översättare** (*translator*), **författare** (*writer*), **läkare** (*doctor*).

There are many exceptions: **konservator** (*art restorer*), **tolk** (*interpreter*), **bibliotekarie** (*librarian*), **kassör** (*cashier*).

The feminine ending **-ska** is less frequent than it used to be, but **sjuksköterska** (*nurse*) refers to both women and men.

Reading and writing

1 Read what Gustav Eriksson writes about himself. Then describe yourself by stating your name and background, your parents, your spouse and children, your job, what sports you like to take part in, your recreational interests, your travels etc.

Det här är jag *This is me*

Hej, jag heter Gustav Eriksson. Jag föddes den 10 februari 1973. Min fru Sofia kommer från Grekland. Vår son heter Magnus och vår dotter Ingrid.

Vi bor i en förort till Stockholm. Jag pendlar varje dag till mitt arbete som snickare. Sofia är sjuksköterska och jobbar på ett sjukhus.

Vi bor i ett trevligt radhusområde (group of semi-detached houses) med bra grannar. På sommaren åker vi till vårt sommarställe i skärgården. Där kan vi bada, fiska och åka båt.

På vintern åker jag skidor och skridskor. Sofia tycker om att laga mat. Hennes favoritmat är stekt strömming med lingonsylt.

Nu vet du mycket om mig! Berätta om dig själv!!!

This is a sign for rules on the beach:
Badregler
Dyk inte på okänt vatten (*Don't dive into unknown waters*).
Varning för starka strömmar (*Strong currents*).
Bada endast mellan de röda flaggorna (*Swim between the flags only*).
Lämna inte barn utan uppsikt (*Don't leave your children unattended*).

The herrings in the Baltic are either called **sill** (in the south) or **strömming** (further north). **Stekt sill** in the southern parts of Sweden is thus called **stekt strömming** further north – but pickled herring is always **inlagd sill**: **sherrysill**, **löksill** (*with onions*), **senapssill** (*with mustard*) etc.

Det här är mina vänner *These are my friends*

Hej, jag heter Jytte. Jag kommer från Danmark och talar danska, svenska, engelska och spanska. Jag besöker mina föräldrar tre gånger om året. Jag är översättare, tolk och lärare.

Jag heter Cecilia. Jag kommer från Sverige men bor i Boston i Amerika. Jag talar svenska, engelska och franska. Jag jobbar som konservator och är i Sverige vartannat år (*every second year*).

Maria heter jag, och jag bor i Stockholm. Jag är journalist på en stor tidning. Nästan varje vecka åker jag till London. Jag gillar att resa.

Jag heter Kristoffer och bor med min familj i Malmö. Jag är bibliotekarie och tar pendeltåget mellan Malmö och Lund varje dag. Jag arbetar på Lunds universitetsbibliotek.

Jag heter Marguerite och bor utanför Stockholm. Jag har tre små barn så jag är hemma-mamma. Två gånger om året åker vi till min mans släktingar på landet.

Test yourself

1 What is the most common ending of nouns for professions?

2 Match the Swedish and the English.

a	barnkammare	**1**	carpets
b	tvättstuga	**2**	suburb
c	vardagsrum	**3**	walls
d	förort	**4**	nursery
e	radhus	**5**	dining area
f	mathörna	**6**	laundry
g	mattor	**7**	living room
h	väggar	**8**	semi-detached house

3 Translate into English.

a Hon sätter sig i soffan.
b Hon lägger sig på mattan.
c De tvättar sig före middagen.
d Hon satt i soffan
e Han låg på mattan.
f De tvättade sig innan de åt middag.

SELF CHECK

	I CAN...
○	... describe a house.
○	... describe myself.
○	... use different tenses.
○	... use reflexive pronouns.

9 Fritidsaktiviteter

Hobbies and free time activities

In this unit you will learn how to:

- ***talk about sport.***
- ***talk about hobbies.***
- ***write a review of a book or a film.***
- ***turn words into their opposites.***

CEFR: (A2) *Can identify the main points of TV news items. Can give simple descriptions or presentations as a short series of simple phrases linked into a list.*

Sport

The fifth Olympic Games were held in Stockholm in 1912. Stockholms Stadion, the splendid venue built for that event, is still used for **landskamper** (*international matches*), not least when the friendly rivalry with Finland is settled in Finnkampen. Nearby is Kungliga Tennishallen, one of the many arenas where Björn Borg (b. 1956) excelled – he won the Wimbledon final on six consecutive years. Part of the Davis Cup is played in Båstad, a small town in the southwest. **Vintersporter** (*winter sports*) like **skidåkning** (*skiing*) and **ishockey** (*ice hockey*) attract many Swedes, as do **vattensporter** (*water sports*) like **simning** (*swimming*) and **segling** (*sailing*). Golf, once an exclusive sport, has become very popular, with an ever increasing number of **golfbanor** (*golf courses*). **Fotboll** (*football*) is the most popular sport. When Sweden reached the World Cup final in 1958, Swedes bought TV sets like never before (Brazil won). The year after, Ingemar Johansson became **världsmästare** (*world champion*) in **boxning** (*boxing*). Zlatan Ibrahimovic (b. 1981) from Malmö is the current Swedish football hero.

Some sport terms have been left untranslated in Swedish, like speedway, motorcross, rally, rugby, curling, badminton, basket, bowling and boules. Others are easily identified when you know that **hopp** means *jump and* **lopp** *race*. What are the following: **höjdhopp, längdhopp, cykellopp, skidlopp**?

Vocabulary builder

09.01 Look at the words and phrases and complete the missing English expressions. Then listen and try to imitate the pronunciation of the speakers.

SPORTS AND HOBBIES	
tennisbana	______
ridlektion	*riding lessons*
gymnastik	*PE in schools*
inneaktivitet	*indoor activity*
bokcirkel	______
ta en promenad	*go for a walk*
dataspel	*computer games*
schack	*chess*
akvarellmålning	*watercolour painting*
körsång	*choir practice*
matlagning	*cooking*
gå på gymmet	______

NEW EXPRESSIONS	
helg	*holiday*
tokig i	*mad about*
schema	*timetable*
aktuell	*topical, recent*

Conversation 1

09.02 *Johan and Magnus discuss what they and their families have been doing over the weekend.*

1 What different sporting activities are mentioned in this conversation?

Johan	Hej Magnus, vad gjorde du i helgen?
Magnus	Hej du, jo, jag såg Båstad-tennisen på teve, och hann med en runda på golfbanan.
Johan	Härligt! Jag tog barnen till ridlektionen.
Magnus	Vad mer är de intresserade av?
Johan	Fotboll, förstås, Zlatan, Zlatan, vår hjälte. Och på vintern är det slalom och ishockey. De lär sig mycket i skolan. På gymnastiken spelar de handboll.
Magnus	Britta, din fru, är hon lika sportintresserad?
Johan	Nej, när vi är ute stannar hon gärna inne. Hon gillar att läsa en god bok, och så brukar hon alltid laga något extra gott till middag på lördagen.
Magnus	Karin är med i en bokcirkel där de diskuterar böcker och aktuella filmer. Och så tar hon gärna en promenad med hunden.
Johan	Din dotter, Anna, vad gillar hon?
Magnus	Tja, det är mest kompisar som gäller. De spelar en massa dataspel.
Johan	Ja, min Henrik är ju klassens schackmästare. Han slår mig nu!
Magnus	Hälsa familjen! Hej hej!
Johan	Tack, detsamma! Hej då!

2 Read the conversation once more and answer the following questions.

a What did Magnus watch on TV?
b Where did Johan take the children?
c What does Britta do when it's quiet at home?
d What are they doing in Karin's book club?

Language discovery

1 ADVERBS

Adverbs often answer the questions **när** (*when*), **var** (*where*) and **hur** (*how*).

Jag lägger mig tidigt. Hon är ute. Han ser dåligt på natten.

Some adverbs are negations, like **inte** (*not*) and **aldrig** (*never*).

Most adverbs end in **-t** in Swedish (and *-ly* in English).

Some end in **-ligen** or **-vis**: **vanligen** (*usually*), **troligen** (*probably*), **delvis** (*partly*), **naturligtvis** (*naturally*).

2 OPPOSITES

When you want to turn a word into its opposite, you most often use the prefix **-o**:

vanlig (*usual, common*) – **ovanlig** (*unusual, uncommon*)

There are many exceptions to this rule, like **aktuell** – **inaktuell**, **populär** – **impopulär**, **respektfull** – **respektlös** (*disrespectful*).

Britta spelade piano. *Britta played the piano.*

Unlike English, Swedish has no definite article here: **Johan spelar trummor**, **Magnus spelar klarinett**, **Karin spelar gitarr**.

Jag går ofta på bio. *I often go to the cinema.*

Likewise, Swedish has no definite article in phrases like these: **Britta går på teater**, **Magnus går på konsert**, **Johan går på rockfestival**.

Practice

1 Put an adverb in front of the adjectives in these sentences. The first has been done for you.

- **a** Han är lång – Han är ovanligt lång
- **b** Greta Garbo var _______ (*unbelievably*) vacker.
- **c** ABBA är fortfarande _______ (*fantastically*) populära.
- **d** Filmen var _______ (*immensely*) intressant.
- **e** Som musiker var Magnus _______ (*colossally*) omtyckt.

2 Write the opposites of the following adjectives.

- **a** bekväm (so that it means *uncomfortable*)
- **b** trevlig (so that it means *unfriendly*)
- **c** intressant (so that it means *uninteresting*)
- **d** gärna (so that it means *unwillingly*)
- **e** gilla (so that it means *dislike*)

ABBA

Like IKEA, the equally *successful* (**framgångsrika**) ABBA is an acronym. Its four members Agneta Fältskog, Björn Ulvaeus, Benny Andersson and Anni-Frid Lyngstad started their group in 1974 and had their *breakthrough* (**genombrott**) with *Waterloo* at the Eurovision Song Contest two years later. Their *records* (**skivor**) have sold in formidable numbers ever since, and their popularity has *never ceased* (**upphört**). Since the *quartet* (**kvartetten**) broke up, Björn Ulvaeus and Benny Andersson became *involved* (**inblandade**) in films and musicals, *among them* (**bland andra**) *Mamma Mia!* and *Chess. Kristina från Duvemåla*, a musical based on Vilhelm Moberg's four *novels* (**romaner**) about 19th century Swedish emigration (**utvandring**) to America, was set to music by Benny Andersson, drawing on Swedish *folk tunes* (**folkmelodier**). *ABBA – The Museum* opened in Stockholm in May 2013.

Köra (*to drive*) is pronounced with an initial soft sound, according to the general rule of **k** in front of **i**, **e**, **y**, **ä** and **ö**. **Kör** (*choir*) is an exception. It is pronounced with an initial hard **k**-sound, as it is a loan word (from the French *chœur* and the Latin *chorus*).

VOCABULARY

09.03

dokumentär	*documentary film*
andra världskriget	*Second World War*
behöva	*need*
omväxling	*variety*
körövning	*choir practice*
omtyckt	*well liked*
världsberömd	*world famous*
utantill	*by heart*
Det var tider det!	*Those were the days!*

Conversation 2

09.04 *Karin and Britta talk about film and music.*

1 Do they have the same interests?

Karin	Jag går ofta på bio. Igår såg jag en väldigt intressant dokumentär om andra världskriget.
Britta	Jag gillar inte dokumentärer. Jag ser hellre komedier. Då blir man lite glad!
Karin	Javisst, man kan behöva det också. Men jag jobbade i trädgården hela dagen och på kvällen behövde jag lite omväxling.
Britta	Jag var på körövning. Vi sjöng vårsånger och det lät otroligt bra. Vi övar varje vecka.
Karin	Så trevligt! Jag brukade sjunga i kör när jag gick i skolan men nu hinner jag inte.
Britta	Jag spelade piano i många år men slutade med det och började sjunga i stället.
Karin	Magnus var med i ett band som spelade dansmusik och de var kolossalt omtyckta.
Britta	Tänk så fantastiskt populära Abba var! De blev ju världsberömda!
Karin	Ja, man kunde de flesta av deras sånger utantill! Det var tider det!

2 Listen to the conversation once more and answer these questions.

a Why does Britta like comedies?

b What kind of songs did they sing at the choir practice?

c How often do they practise?

d What instrument did Britta play before joining the choir?

3 Find four adverbs in the conversation, all ending in -t.

VOCABULARY

09.05

fortsätta	*continue*
Götaland, Svealand, Norrland	*southern Sweden, central Sweden, northern Sweden*
åska	*thunder*
sval	*cool*
regnområde	*rain area*
överlägsen	*superior*
målskytt	*scorer*
mål	*goal*
målvakt	*goalkeeper*
halvlek	*half*
passning	*pass*
försvar	*defence*
straff	*penalty*
chanslös	*without a chance*

Listening

09.06 **Listen to this weather forecast taken from a television news programme.**

Väderleksrapport för hela landet.

Det varma vädret fortsätter i Götaland med temperaturer över tjugofem grader och med risk för åska. Svealand får ostadigt väder med moln och svalare vindar. Över det mesta av Norrland drar ett regnområde in från nordväst.

What is the weather forecast for the following?

a Götaland
b Svealand
c Norrland

Reading 1

FOTBOLLSREFERAT I EN DAGSTIDNING *SUMMARY OF A FOOTBALL MATCH IN A DAILY PAPER*

Zlatan igen! Sverige vann överlägset med 4–0 över England i söndagens fotbollslandskamp i Göteborg. Zlatan var matchens store målskytt, han gjorde kvällens alla mål. Det första målet kom redan i andra minuten av första halvlek, på en passning från Henke Larsson. Det andra dröjde tio minuter in i andra halvlek, efter en hörna. Det tredje kom två minuter senare när Zlatan var fri från engelska försvaret, och det fjärde kom en minut före full tid på en straff. Den engelske målvakten var chanslös!

Translate the following sentences into English.

a Zlatan gjorde kvällens alla mål.
b Det första målet kom efter en passning från Henke Larsson.
c Det fjärde målet kom en minut före full tid på en straff.
d Den engelske målvakten var chanslös.

INGMAR BERGMAN (1918–2007)

Smiles of a Summer Night, a delightful comedy loosely based on Shakespeare's *A Midsummer Night's Dream*, won a prize at the 1955 Cannes film festival for Ingmar Bergman. A long series of internationally acclaimed films and TV dramas followed, among them *The Seventh Seal* (an apocalyptic allegory set in the time of the Black Death), the trilogy *Through a Glass Darkly*, *Winter Light* and *The Silence* (which had problems with censorship), and *Scenes from a Marriage* (a sophisticated domestic drama series). The epic *Fanny and Alexander*, set in Bergman's native city Uppsala, confronts the joyful theatrical Ekdahl family (the surname borrowed from Ibsen's drama *The Wild Duck*) with the forbidding and ascetic bishop Vergérus (Bergman's father was a Lutheran pastor). Throughout his long artistic life, Bergman was also a prolific theatre director.

VOCABULARY

09.07

läkare *(medical) doctor*
fira *celebrate*
disputera *defend a doctoral thesis*
smultronstället *the wild strawberry patch*
liftare *hitchhiker*

försonas med *come to terms with*

skådespelare *actor*

filmregissör *film director*

huvudroll *main character*

Reading 2

EN FILMRECENSION *A FILM REVIEW*

I filmregissören Ingmar Bergmans Smultronstället (Wild Strawberries) från 1957 kör den gamle läkaren Isak Borg i sin stora Packard-bil från Stockholm ner till universitetet i Lund för att fira att det är femtio år sedan han disputerade. Med sig i bilen har han sin sons hustru, och på vägen ner tar de upp tre liftare också. Han reser både i rummet (Sverige på sommaren i vackra bilder) och i tiden (i tre olika drömmar konfronteras han med traumatiska episoder i sitt liv). När resan är slut förstår han sig själv bättre och försonas med sitt liv. Det är en mycket bra film, med den legendariske skådespelaren Victor Sjöström i huvudrollen.

Answer the following questions.

a Why does Isak Borg drive down to Lund?
b Four people come along with him in the car. Who are they?
c What time of the year is it?
d Who directed the film, and who played the leading role?

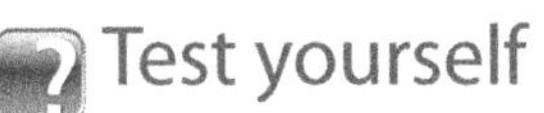

Test yourself

1 Answer the following questions in Swedish.

a Vilka sorts filmer tycker du om att se?
b Spelar du något instrument?
c Tycker du om att sjunga?
d Vad gjorde du förra helgen?

2 Write a summary of a football match, or a review of a film or a book.

3 Match the following words with their opposites.

a inne	**1** ledsen
b ofta	**2** tragedi
c vinter	**3** ute
d glad	**4** dålig
e komedi	**5** sommar
f bra	**6** sällan

SELF CHECK

	I CAN...
○	... talk about sports.
○	... talk about hobbies.
○	... review a book or a film.
○	... turn adjectives into adverbs.

Svenska högtider och fester

Holidays and festivities in Sweden

In this unit you will learn how to:

- ***greet each other on the different holidays of the year.***
- ***use prepositions of time and place.***
- ***use the passive form of the verb.***
- ***use demonstrative pronouns.***

CEFR: (A2) *Can write short, simple notes and messages relating to matters in areas of immediate needs.*

Swedish holidays

There are many occasions to celebrate holidays and festivals in the course of a year. The first day of January is **Nyårsdagen** (*New Year's Day*). **Påsk** (*Easter*) is celebrated with the individual days known as **skärtorsdag**, **långfredag**, **påskafton**, **påskdagen** and **annandag påsk**. Bonfires are lit on **Valborgsmässoafton** on 30 April. **Första maj** is the international *Labour Day* on 1 May, while **Nationaldagen** is a specific Swedish holiday on 6 June, also called **Svenska flaggans dag**. **Midsommarafton** (always on a Friday) is on or near the summer solstice at the end of June. **Allhelgonadagen** in November is *All Saints' Day* while **Lucia** is celebrated on 13 December. Then comes **Jul** (*Christmas*). **Julklapparna** (*the Christmas gifts*) are given on **Julafton** (*Christmas Eve*) not on **Juldagen** (*Christmas Day*). **Annandag jul** is *Boxing Day*, and finally, on **Nyårsafton** (*New Year's Eve*), the new year is celebrated with **fyrverkerier** (*fireworks*).

Every fourth year is a **skottår**, with February 29 as a **skottdag**.

How would you say these words in English?

HOLIDAY GREETINGS

Till jul säger vi GOD JUL (*Merry Christmas*) till varandra. På nyåret önskar vi varandra ett GOTT NYTT ÅR (*Happy New Year*). Sedan kommer GLAD PÅSK (*Happy Easter*). Och i slutet av juni GLAD MIDSOMMAR (*Happy Midsummer*). Och när någon fyller år önskar man GLAD FÖDELSEDAG (*Happy birthday*) eller GRATTIS PÅ FÖDELSEDAGEN. (*Congratulations on your birthday*). GRATTIS är en förkortning av GRATULATIONER. Och kanske har man en namnsdag att fira? GRATTIS PÅ NAMNSDAGEN! (*Happy nameday*). I slutet av veckan kan man önska varandra TREVLIG HELG (*Have a nice weekend*), och i slutet av dagen GOD NATT. Nästa morgon blir det GOD MORGON, och när man äter sin middag SMAKLIG MÅLTID (*Bon appétit*).

Vocabulary builder

10.01 **Look at the words and expressions. Listen and try to imitate their pronunciation.**

CHRISTMAS

adventsljus	*advent candles*
julgran	*Christmas tree*
julotta	*the church service very early on Christmas Day*

NEW EXPRESSIONS

doft	*smell, fragrance*
spänning	*thrill*
snäll	*kind, well-behaved*
utdelning	*handing out*
snöig	*snowy*
glögg	*mulled wine*
strålande	*radiant*
älska	*love*

Conversation 1

10.02 *Adam and Eva talk about festivities in December.*

1 How do they cope with the darkness?

Adam	Snart har vi december, julmånaden. Jag gillar det här mörkret och de här korta dagarna.
Eva	Ja, man håller sig hellre inomhus än utomhus, ljusen tänds, man dricker varm glögg. Och har man tur kommer det snö på julaftonen!
Adam	Det firas mycket i december! Nobeldagen den 10 december och Lucia den 13 december. Och sedan är det inte långt till jul.
Eva	Vi tänder våra adventsljus varje söndag, och till den 24 december har vi tänt alla fyra. Då ska julgranen skaffas. Det är härligt med doften av gran i vardagsrummet!
Adam	Julaftonsmorgon, med ljus i alla fönster, med julklappar under granen, med doft av julmat, med spänningen och väntan på JULTOMTEN!
Eva	'Finns här några snälla barn?' Javisst! Vi har alla varit SÅ snälla hela året! Och så börjar julklappsutdelningen.
Adam	Julaftonskvällen är speciell; mörker, ljus och julsånger. Många vuxna går i midnattsmässan och vandrar hem genom snöiga gator och känner att nu är det jul!
Eva	Fortfarande är det många, speciellt de äldre, som av tradition går i julottan på juldagsmorgonen.
Adam	'Jul, jul, strålande jul.' Vi älskar de där traditionerna!

2 Fill in the missing prepositions in the following sentences.

a Man håller sig hellre _______ än _______.

b Har man tur kommer det snö _______ julaftonen.

c Sedan är det inte långt _______ påsk.

d Det är härligt med doften _______ gran _______ vardagsrummet.

e Julaftonsmorgon, _______ ljus _______ alla fönster och julklappar _______ granen.

f Vi vandrar hem _______ snöiga gator.

g Många går _______ julottan _______ juldagsmorgonen.

Language discovery

1 PREPOSITIONS OF PLACE

Some prepositions show where something is or takes place.

i (*in*), **på** (*on*), **vid** (*at*), **under** (for place = *under*, for time = *during*), **över** (*over*), **framför** (*in front of*), **bakom** (*behind*), **genom** (*through*). Note **gå i skolan, kyrkan** (*go to school, church*) and **arbeta på ett kontor** (*work in an office*). **På** is used for islands: **jag bor på Gotland, Nya Zeeland, Island, Grönland** (*I live in Gotland, New Zealand, Iceland, Greenland*) unless they are continents: **han bor i Australien**.

2 PREPOSITIONS OF TIME

Some prepositions show when something happens.

a) For something that will happen in the future you use the following: **på torsdag, på lördag** (*on Thursday, on Saturday*); **i morgon, i jul, i påsk** (*tomorrow, this coming Christmas, this coming Easter*); **om en timme**, **om en kvart**, **om en stund** (*in an hour, in 15 minutes, in a while*).

b) For something that happened in the past you use: **i torsdags**, **i lördags**, **i går**, **i julas**, **i påskas** (*last Thursday, last Saturday, yesterday, last Christmas, last Easter*); **för en timme sedan**, **för en kvart sedan**, **för en stund sedan** (*an hour ago, 15 minutes ago, a while ago*).

3 VERBS IN THE PASSIVE

The passive is used to say that something happened to something or someone (as opposed to the active that says someone did something).

Cykeln stals av tjuven, cykeln blev stulen av tjuven.	*The bike was stolen by the thief.*

The passive form of the verb is expressed either with an added **-s** or with the help of the verbs **att vara** (*to be*) or **att bli** (*to become*): **Tjuven fångades av polisen. Tjuven blev fångad av polisen** (*The thief was caught by the police*).

Note that a few verbs have the **-s** form without the passive meaning, among them **andas** (*breathe*), **hoppas** (*hope*), **lyckas** (*succeed*), **finnas** (*exist*).

4 DEMONSTRATIVE PRONOUNS

Denna, detta (*this one*) and **dessa** (*these*) are followed by a noun in the indefinite form. **Den här**, **det här** (*this one*), **de här** (*these*), **den där**, **det där** (*that one*), **de där** (*those*) are followed by a noun in the definite form:

Denna bok/den här boken är min present till dig. Detta hus/det här huset bodde jag i som barn. Dessa foton/de här fotona är på min syster. Den där boken är din. Det där huset är nybyggt. De där fotona på min syster togs av mig.

Practice

Translate the underlined words into Swedish.

- **a** The dog is under the table during dinner.
- **b** I walk through the town.
- **c** She drove to Stockholm an hour ago.
- **d** He came to Sweden last summer.
- **e** The Christmas tree was bought by dad.
- **f** The candles are lit every Sunday.
- **g** Those shoes are comfortable.
- **h** This house is mine.

VOCABULARY

10.03

anlända	*arrive*
semester	*holidays*
bröllop	*wedding*
höjdpunkt	*highlight*
kräftfest	*crayfish party*
smyga	*creep, sneak*
hedra	*honour, celebrate*
längta efter	*long for*

Conversation 2

10.04 *Carl and Karin talk about what to celebrate throughout the year.*

Which summer celebrations are mentioned, and which winter ones?

Carl	Vi svenskar är faktiskt mycket traditionella av oss. Hela december, julmånaden, är min favoritmånad, med Nobeldagen den 10 december, Lucia den 13 december och julaftonen den 24 december. Vilken helg är din favorit?
Karin	Påsken! Den är alltid välkommen i vårmånaden april, och jag tycker ju så mycket om ägg, både riktiga hönsägg och chokladägg! Man känner att vintern är slut och att våren är här!
Carl	Många har midsommaren som favorit, då sommaren riktigt har anlänt och de flesta redan har semester eller börjar industrisemestern i juli. Och ett riktigt sommarbröllop på midsommaraftonen, det är så romantiskt!
Karin	Absolut! Sommarens höjdpunkter, och sedan kräftfest i augusti, då mörkret smyger in igen.
Carl	En vacker högtid är också Alla helgons dag tidigt i november, med tända ljus på alla gravar för att minnas och hedra våra döda släktingar och vänner.
Karin	Då har vintermörkret kommit, och då börjar vi redan längta efter nästa sommar, med långa ljusa nätter!

Speaking

10.05 **Listen to the conversation once more, then play the part of Karin in the following dialogue.**

Carl	Vilken helg är din favorit?
Karin	*I like Easter because I like eggs, both from hens and the chocolate eggs.*
Carl	Midsommar är min favorithelg och ett sommarbröllop på midsommarafton är romantiskt.
Karin	*Absolutely. The crayfish parties in August are also one of the highlights in summer.*
Carl	På allhelgonadagen tänder vi ljus på gravarna.
Karin	*And then we long for the long white summer nights!*

NEW WORDS

är kommen	*har kommit*
rund	*globe*
glimma, glänsa	*shine*
stall	*stable*
fjärran	*far away*
hägring	*mirage, illusion*
fägring	*beauty*

Reading 1

Christmas is the darkest time of the year, with the winter solstice on 21 December. Many of the traditional Christmas songs and carols contrast light and darkness, as apparent in the underlined words:

1 **Nu har vi ljus här i vårt hus. Julen är kommen…**

2 **Nu tändas tusen juleljus på jordens mörka rund…**

3 **När juldagsmorgon glimmar, jag vill till stallet gå…**

4 **Gläns över sjö och strand, stjärna ur fjärran…**

5 **Sankta Lucia, ljusklara hägring, sprid i vår vinternatt glans av din fägring…**

NEW WORDS

uppfinnare	*inventor*
industriman	*industrialist*
förmögenhet	*wealth*
årlig	*annual*
dödsdag	*day of death*
dela ut	*award*

upplösa *dissolve*
instifta *establish*
till minne av *in memory of*
riksbank *national bank of Sweden*
fortfarande *still*
kemi *chemistry*
fysik *physics*
fred *peace*

Reading 2

Read the text on the six Nobel prizes, then answer the questions that follow.

NOBELPRISERNA

Kemisten, uppfinnaren och industrimannen Alfred Nobel (1833–98) testamenterade en del av sin enorma förmögenhet (den kom från hans patent på dynamit) till fem årliga priser, i kemi, fysik, medicin, litteratur och fred. På hans dödsdag den tionde december, Nobeldagen, delas sedan 1901 de fyra första priserna ut i Stockholm, och det femte, fredspriset, i Oslo i Norge. På Nobels tid var Sverige och Norge en union som upplöstes 1905, sju år efter hans död. Ett sjätte pris instiftades 1968, ekonomipriset till Alfred Nobels minne. Då fyllde Sveriges Riksbank trehundra år. Den är världens äldsta riksbank som fortfarande existerar.

a Where did Alfred Nobel get his money from?
b How many prizes are handed out in Sweden, and how many in Oslo?
c One prize is a latecomer. Which one?
d What is the reason behind 10 December being Nobel Day?

Writing

A formal invitation to a New Year's celebration might look like this:

> Härmed inbjuds Petra och Per Persson till nyårsfest med middag och dans.
>
> Klädsel: Frack (tails) eller smoking (tuxedo), festklänning (evening dress).
>
> Tid: Tisdagen den 31 december 2013, kl. 18.00
>
> Plats: Drottninggatan 86, 5 tr. Portkod: 5678.
>
> Välkomna!
>
> Elsa och Erik Eriksson
>
> OSA (om svar anhålles = RSVP) senast 15 december.

1 Reply to Elsa and Erik Eriksson, accepting or declining their invitation.

2 Det här är svaren – vilka är frågorna? Write questions to these answers, using a) vilken, b) när, c) varför, d) vem.

a December är min favoritmånad.
b Den är i vårmånaden april.
c För att hedra de döda.
d Lucia!

Test yourself

1 What are the five days of Easter called in Swedish?

2 What is the Swedish for Father Christmas? On what day does he come with his gifts?

3 Which are the Swedish words for the five original Nobel prizes?

4 What is the lengthy title of the sixth prize? Why was it established in 1968?

SELF CHECK

	I CAN...
○	... talk about Swedish holidays and festivities.
○	... use prepositions of time and place.
○	... use verbs in the passive voice.
○	... use demonstrative pronouns.

R3 Review 3

1 Translate the following sentences into English.

a Ebba får röda tulpaner av Sven på sin födelsedag.
b Per åt köttbullar och potatis till lunch i går.
c Zlatan gjorde tre mål i matchen och den danske målvakten hade inte en chans.
d Översättaren kunde fem språk, tolken kunde sju.
e Boken som låg på bordet ställdes på hyllan av bibliotekarien.
f Journalisten skrev i tidningen om staden som hade klarat sig i jordbävningen.

2 Match the Swedish (a to f) to the English (1 to 6).

a Den extra dagen vart fjärde år kallas skottdag.
b De här fotona är på mina morföräldrar.
c Om svar anhålles senast på måndag.
d Härmed inbjuds du till middag med dans.
e Nu ska vi se vad som finns på matsedeln.
f Kräftfesten är en av sommarens höjdpunkter.

1 RSVP Monday at the latest.
2 Now let's see what's on the menu.
3 These photos are of my mother's parents.
4 The crayfish party is one of the highlights in summer.
5 The added day every four years is called leap day.
6 You are hereby invited to a dinner dance.

3 Fill in the missing forms of these verbs in different tenses.

Tenses	Present	Past	Perfect	Future
baka	bakar	bakade	har bakat	ska baka
bake	*I bake*	*I baked*	*I have baked*	*I shall/will bake*
se	ser	______	______	______
handla	______	handlade	______	______
besöka	______	______	har besökt	______

äta	äter	______	______	______
hälsa	______	______	______	ska hälsa
köpa	köper	______	______	______
gå	______	gick	______	______

4 10.06 **Annika and Johan discuss their hobbies.**
Read the text and answer the questions that follow.

Annika	I går var jag på bio och såg en otroligt bra svensk detektivfilm. Vad gjorde du?
Johan	Jag spelade fotboll på eftermiddagen. Vi tränar varje vecka, alltid på lördagar.
Annika	Spelar alla dina kompisar fotboll?
Johan	Ja, både Erik, Kalle, Mats och Jens är med.
Annika	Vad mer är du intresserad av?
Johan	Jag läser mycket, ofta två böcker i veckan. Vad gör du?
Annika	Ofta läser jag nya deckare, och jag gillar att promenera. Jag har ju en hund som vill ut och gå. Är dina barn sportintresserade?
Johan	Ja. Min dotter Katarina spelar tennis och min son Rufus spelar golf.
Annika	Golf har verkligen blivit kolossalt populärt! Och är inte golfbanorna och golfklubbarna i Sverige fina?
Johan	Jo, absolut! Och vi reser mycket i familjen. Min fru kommer från Frankrike och hon har sina släktingar där.
Annika	Talar du franska?
Johan	Ja det gör jag, inte perfekt men helt acceptabelt.
Annika	Vi reser ofta inom Skandinavien. Både Norge och Danmark är populära länder i vår familj.
Johan	Norge på vintern och Danmark på sommaren?
Annika	Ja, så är det oftast. Då blir det skidor på vintern och bad på sommaren. Vi besöker också de fina konstmuseerna när vi är i Danmark.

a Vad gjorde Annika I går? Och vad gjorde Johan?
b Hur ofta tränar Johan?
c Är hans kompisar också sportintresserade?
d Vad har Johan mer för intressen?
e Och Annika, vad gillar hon?

f Är Sverige ett golf-vänligt land?
g Varför besöker Johan och hans familj ofta Frankrike?
h Vart reser Annika och hennes familj gärna på vintern?
i Vad tycker hon om att göra när hon är i Danmark?

5 10.07 **The family gathers for a Sunday dinner and a catch-up of what has happened during the week. What food do they start the meal with?**

Pappa	Så trevligt att se er alla här. Välkomna till bords!
Magnus	Det luktar gott! Jag är jättehungrig!
Mamma	Smaklig måltid! Vi börjar med lite soppa.
Helene	Den är så god, mamma. Kan jag få receptet?
Mamma	Javisst! Och vad har ni gjort under veckan?
Magnus	Jag har mest studerat nya kurser i ekonomi.
Helene	Och jag har bara jobbat. Att vara lärare är otroligt intensivt!
Pappa	Ja, men snart har du väl jullov. Vad ska du göra då?
Helene	Jo, då ska jag inte tänka på skolan utan bara träffa kompisar.
Magnus	Jag vill också ha jullov! Att läsa ekonomi är så trist.
Mamma	Men med en bra ekonomexamen kan du säkert få ett bra jobb?
Pappa	Det hoppas vi. Och nu börjar vi på den kokta laxen. Skål på er!
Alla	Skål!
Mamma	Och Helene kom med en god efterrätt. Chokladmousse!
Magnus	Jättegott! Så duktigt du är, syrran!
Mamma	Sedan sätter vi oss i soffan och diskuterar vad som händer vecka 46. Vad är planerna?

a Vad äter familjen till förrätt?
b Hur vet vi att Helene gillar mammas soppa?
c Vad har Magnus gjort under veckan?
d Vad är Helenes jobb?
e Vad tänker Helene göra under jullovet?
f Vad säger Magnus om sina studier?
g Vad äter de till efterrätt, och vem har lagat den?
h Vad gör de efter middagen?

6 10.08 **Mats and Esmeralda discuss what to eat for Christmas, and where. Read their conversation and answer the questions.**

Esmeralda	Du Mats, om vi skulle gå ut och äta julbord i år! Det är dyrt, men då får vi smaka alla svenska julspecialiteter!
Mats	Javisst, Esmeralda. Det tycker jag vi gör. Då kan vi själva ha en slimmad julmiddag på julafton.
Esmeralda	Jättebra! Vi tar bara skinka (ham) och rödkål (red cabbage) här hemma.
Mats	Ja, då ska jag äta mig mätt på alla olika sillrätter i restaurangen.
Esmeralda	Vi ringer och bokar i dag. Det är så populärt så det måste vi göra.

a What does Esmeralda suggest to Mats?
b How would her suggestion affect their Christmas dinner?
c What can they not do without at home?
d What does Mats intend to focus on at the restaurant's big **julbord**?
e Do they have to book a table in advance?

7 These are all the first names mentioned in the ten units of the book. Most of them appear in the Nameday calendar in Unit 4 – look up their dates, and learn more Swedish names in the process.

Adam	David	Gustav	Lena	Per
Agneta	Ebba	Göran	Lisbeth	Peter
Alexander	Elin	Hans	Lotta	Petra
Alfred	Elisabeth	Helena	Magnus	Sanna
Anni-Frid	Elsa	Ingmar	Margareta	Sara
Ben	Emma	Jenny	Marguerite	Sofia
Benny	Erik	Jens	Maria	Susanna
Björn	Esmeralda	Johan	Mary	Sven
Bonnie	Eva	Jytte	Mats	Torsten
Britta	Fanny	Karin	Olav	Ulla
Carl	Filip	Kerstin	Oskar	Ulrika
Cecilia	Fredrik	Kristoffer	Patrik	Victor

Answer key

UNIT 1

Greetings

Good morning, good afternoon (or just hello), good evening, good night

Vocabulary builder

Hello; How are you?

Conversation 1

1 Hej; Hej då

2 a She is going to London; **b** She is a computer consultant; **c** He is a journalist; **d** She lives in Stockholm

Language discovery

1 a Jag är journalist; **b** Var flyger du till? or Vart flyger du?

2 a Jag heter Ben Anderson; **b** Jag bor i New York; present tense of the verb ends in -r

3 a Vad?; **b** Var?

Practice

1 a – 3; **b** – 5; **c** – 2; **d** – 4; **e** – 6; **f** – 7; **g** – 8; **h** – 1

2 a Jag är svensk; **b** Du bor i New York; **c** Hon möter honom i Amerika; **d** Jag mår bra; **e** De går till gaten

3 a – 3; **b** – 4; **c** – 5; **d** – 2; **e** – 1

Conversation 2

1 Filip is a football coach; Oskar is an engineer

2 a His job is quite OK; **b** He earns enough for him and his family; **c** If he can get a babysitter; **d** Filip will buy the tickets

Speaking

Oskar: Tjena Filip! Hur är läget?
Filip: Jag mår bra. Och du?
Oskar: Jo tack, det knallar. Vad gör du nuförtiden?
Filip: Jag jobbar som fotbollstränare. Vad gör du?

Oskar: Jag har ett hyfsat jobb som ingenjör.
Filip: Låter kul. Hyfsat betalt?
Oskar: Tja, lagom för att klara familjen.
Filip: Hänger du med på bio på torsdag?
Oskar: Gärna, om jag kan ordna barnvakt.
Filip: Jag fixar biljetterna så ses vi där. Ha det bra till dess.
Oskar: Du med. Hej på dej.

Reading

a Waiting for planes to New York and London; **b** No, they exchange names and numbers; **c** She will phone Ben

Writing

a Jag ska hämta barnen på dagis; **b** Hänger du med på bio på torsdag?; **c** Gärna om jag kan ordna barnvakt

Test yourself

1 a Hon reser till London; **b** Jag är journalist; **c** Jag heter Lisbeth Wallander och jag bor i Stockholm

2 a Henne; **b** Vi; **c** Oss; **d** Ni

3 a Var bor du?; **b** Vad heter du?; **c** Hur mår du?

4 a Hej; **b** God morgon; **c** God natt

UNIT 2

Relatives

Sonson and sondotter; Fäder och söner

Vocabulary builder

Maternal grandparents, paternal grandparents, winter, summer

Conversation 1

1 The grandparents look after the children.
2 a He is at the daycare centre; **b** Susanna takes him there, his father collects him; **c** Maternal and paternal grandparents; **d** Her relatives live further away
3 a – 4; **b** – 5; **c** – 2; **d** – 1; **e** – 3
4 dagar, kusiner

Practice

1 a skor; **b** familjer; **c** bin; **d** jobb; **e** dagar; **f** kronor
3 a Ja, det är det; **b** Jo, det är det; **c** Jo, det är han; **d** Ja, det är hon; **e** Ja, det är det; **f** Jo, det är det.

Conversation 2

It's minus 10 degrees.

Speaking

3 Kerstin:	Hej Göran, i dag biter det i skinnet.
Göran:	Ja, det är kallt, minus tio grader, men det är skönt att åka skidor.
Kerstin:	Ja, det är skönt. Vad gör du i morgon?
Göran:	Om jag kan starta bilen kör jag till Göteborg. Kommer du med?
Kerstin:	Det kan jag inte, jag flyger till Kina och Nya Zeeland.

Reading

1 a They meet outside the kindergarten; **b** No, it is a long time since they met; **c** She has left Pelle there; **d** Also at the kindergarten; **e** She will buy food for dinner.
2 Parents, maternal grandmother, maternal grandfather, paternal grandmother, paternal grandfather, siblings, maternal aunt, maternal uncle, paternal aunt, paternal uncle, son, daughter, sister, brother, cousin, wife, brother-in-law, sister-in-law, second cousin, children
3 a They are cousins; **b** They are sisters-in-law; **c** They are cousins; **d** They are second cousins; **e** They are brothers-in-law

Test yourself

1 a Kusiner; **b** Mödrar; **c** Syskon
2 vår, sommar, höst, vinter
3 a Vi har släktingar i Amerika; **b** Jag är gift med Eva. Hon är min fru; **c** Anna är min äldre syster.
4 a Ja, det är kallt; **b** Nej, det är inte kallt.

UNIT 3

Hotels in Sweden

Non-smoking room, WiFi, wake-up call, night porter, air conditioning

Vocabulary builder

Single room, bathroom, card payment, front desk

Conversation 1

1 The price of the double room; the check-in and check-out times; that their granddaughter can stay there as well
2 a They are in Stockholm for six days; **b** Check-in and check-out are both at noon; **c** Their granddaughter
3 a – 3; **b** – 4; **c** – 5; **d** – 2; **e** – 1
4 Är frukosten inkluderad? Ja, frukosten är inkluderad.
5 a Nu är vi här; **b** Nu ska vi utforska Stockholm

Practice

1 a Går vi in?; **b** Har vi alltid sen utcheckning?; **c** Kostar det 780 kronor?; **d** Det går bra; **e** Frukosten ingår; **f** Hon är fem år
2 a Då tar vi rummet; **b** Då är hon så välkommen; **c** Nu utforskar de Stockholm; **d** Då vill han lämna resväskorna; **e** Då måste du hitta ett trevligt hotell; **f** Nu ska jag se vad jag kan erbjuda.
3 a femtio; **b** sextio; **c** sjuttiofem; **d** tjugofem

Language discovery

Onsdag, torsdag, fredag, måndag

Speaking

Emma:	Kan vi boka ett dubbelrum?
Portiern:	Ja, vi har ett dubbelrum med utsikt över Gamla Stan.
Erik:	Hur mycket kostar det?
Portiern:	Det kostar 780 kronor.
Erik:	Var är hissen?
Portiern:	Hissen är där borta till höger
Erik:	På vilken våning är rummet?
Portiern:	Rummet är på första våningen.

Pronunciation

Quite an advantage, as you stay for free

Conversation 2

1 Name, nationality, address, phone number
2 a Blandäktenskap; **b** Det skulle vara allt; **c** Hissen är där borta till höger; **d** Alla rum har rökförbud/Alla rum är rökfria; **e** jag hoppas ni får en trevlig tid/vistelse i Stockholm.

Reading

1 a WiFi; **b** design; **c** star; **d** sauna

2 a TV and WiFi; **b** In Scandinavia; **c** View of the water; **d** You can use a gym, a sauna and often a swimming pool.

Test yourself

1 a Jag reser till Stockholm på torsdag; **b** Han bokar ett hotellrum från onsdag till söndag; **c** Min dotter kommer på tisdag.

2 a Kaffe kostar femton och en kaka sex, det blir tjugoen kronor, tack; **b** Mitt telefonnummer är femtiosju sextiotre tjugoåtta; **c** Landskoden för Sverige är noll noll fyrtiosex.

3 a Är Ebba professor i kemi?; **b** Bor hon hos oss när hon är i Lund?; **c** Är vi deras gäster?; **d** Är det gratis för henne att bo hos oss?

R1 (UNITS 1–3)

1 a Sweden, Norway and Denmark; **b** Sweden, Norway, Denmark, Finland and Iceland; **c** Finland and Iceland; **d** Sweden, Norway and Denmark; **e** Stockholm, Oslo, Copenhagen, Helsingfors/Helsinki, Reykjavik

2 Moster, morbror, mormor, morfar – faster, farbror, farmor, farfar

3 a Sofia and her sisters live in Malmö, Ivan and his brothers in Moscow; **b** Sofia is a nurse, Ivan is studying to become a doctor; **c** Her mother is a pilot, her father a nuclear scientist. His mother is an engineer and his father a professor of Scandinavian languages; **d** Kastrup is the Copenhagen/København airport, reached from Malmö via the bridge across Öresund.

4 Sofia and her family: tjugofyra, tjugosju, nitton, femtiosex, femtioåtta; Ivan and his brothers: tjugosex, trettio, tjugotre

5 When saying hello and goodbye, Sofia uses the less formal hej and hej då, Ivan the more formal god dag and adjö

UNIT 4

Paying

Welcome; insert your card; enter your pin number; choose amount; press WITHDRAWAL; take your card; take your money; welcome back

Vocabulary builder

Green, red, blue, brown, orange, hat, belt, bakery, price tag

Conversation 1

1 Buying clothes bores him

2 a He thinks it is boring; **b** He needs brown walking shoes, size 45; **c** Only one pair; **d** With the receipt, the shoes can be exchanged
3 Skor, kläder, skoaffär, kvitto
4 a – 3; **b** – 4; **c** – 1; **d** – 5; **e** – 2

Practice

1 En dag, en katt, en hund are non-neuter; ett lejon, ett djur, ett rum, ett stearinljus are neuter
2 Katt – katten – katter – katterna; Lejon – lejonet – lejon – lejonen; Hund – hunden – hundar – hundarna; Djur – djuret – djur – djuren; Rum – rummet – rum – rummen; Stearinljus – stearinljuset – stearinljus – stearinljusen
3 Kvinnor, möbler, tändstickor, smycken, böcker, skor, bin, män
4 Kvinnor: för kläder fyrtio till fyrtiotvå och för skor trettiosex. Män: för kläder femtiofyra till femtiosex och för skor fyrtiotvå.

Speaking

Sofia: Jag behöver faktiskt titta på lite nya kläder
Jenny: Vi börjar i det stora varuhuset. Där finns mycket att välja på.
Sofia: Den här sitter snyggt. Vad tycker du?
Jenny: Jättebra. Har du skor som passar till?

Conversation 2

1 They are looking for clothes and end up buying a dress, a pair of trousers and a sweater
2 a Svart, med vita prickar; **b** Det passar precis; **c** Vi fick rabatt i dag; **d** Vi slapp det otäcka vädret
3 a – 2; **b** – 4; **c** – 5; **d** – 3; **e** – 1

Reading

The washing instructions recommend dry cleaning but it can be washed by hand or in a washing machine in lukewarm water with garments of the same colour, and left to drip-dry – no tumble drying.

Test yourself

1 a Pay cash; **b** Use a credit card; **c** Withdraw money from the cash machine; **d** Use bank notes and coins
2 a Jag vill prova ett par byxor; **b** Jag tycker om den ljusblå färgen; **c** Hur mycket kostar de?; **d** Kan jag betala med kreditkort?
3 a Du behöver verkligen nya skor; **b** Att köpa kläder är trist; **c** Rätt storlek, och jag gillar färgen; **d** Ska du inte prova några andra?

UNIT 5

Travelling in Sweden

There are more cars than car parks. Less traffic also means less pollution.

Vocabulary builder

Return ticket, travel agent, restaurant car, a visit, suggestion, continuation, controller/inspector

Conversation 1

1 Sara and Patrik want to visit their grandparents, an aunt and an uncle, and their cousins. They'll travel by bus and train and then fly back.
2 a Vi tar tåget; **b** Det är snabbare; **c** Vi kan hyra en bil i stället; **d** Resebyrån kollar de andra alternativen
3 a Sara and Patrik; **b** They take the bus; **c** They take the train; **d** They fly back

Practice

1 a Min yngsta syster är sju år yngre än jag/mig (both can be used); **b** Mt Everest är det högsta berget. **c** Tåget till Stockholm är snabbare än bilen; **d** Att cykla är långsammare men bättre; **e** Hon flyger norrut och han söderut; **f** Göteborg är/ligger i väster, Kalmar i öster.
2 a – 6; **b** – 4; **c** – 1; **d** – 5; **e** – 3; **f** – 2
3 a ung; **b** stort; **c** svenska

Conversation 2

1 Ulla is going via Stockholm to Boston; Agneta is going to Stockholm.
2 a För att hälsa på sin dotter; **b** Hon ska fira sin sons födelsedag, ta färjan till Djurgården och äta lunch på Skansen; **c** Kaviar, kaffe och sill.

Speaking

Agneta:	Hej Ulla, vart ska du resa?
Ulla:	Jag flyger till min dotter i Boston
Agneta:	Vad tar du med till henne?
Ulla:	Kaviar, lite sill och svenskt kaffe, mycket starkare än amerikanskt kaffe.
Agneta:	Det är pingstafton i morgon, då fyller min son trettio år.
Ulla:	Min dotter är yngre, hon är tjugofem. Hur firar du hans födelsedag?

Reading

a The 17.58 train arrives at 11.40, the 22.12 one at 16.31; **b** 21 minutes; **c** 54 minutes (11.40 – 12.34) or 48 minutes (16.31 – 17.19); **d** 18.12; **e** Around 24 hours (12.11 – 11.40 or 16.11 – 16.31)

Test yourself

1 a Klockan sex på morgonen; **b** Fem i halv tio på morgonen; **c** Klockan tolv på dagen, mitt på dagen; **d** Kvart i två på eftermiddagen; **e** Halv fem på kvällen; **f** Fem i halv tolv på natten
2 a Högertrafik; **b** Norr, öster; **c** Åka buss eller ta tunnelbanan
3 a Tåget är snabbare än bussen; **b** Det är längre till faster Eva och farbror Hans än till mormor och morfar; **c** Vi kollar vad det kostar att hyra bil; **d** Den gamle mannen är äldre än den gamla kvinnan.

UNIT 6

Stockholm

King, queen, harbour/port, new, main, church, cloister, school, villa

Vocabulary builder

Traffic light, park, parking space, fill the tank, petrol station

Conversation 1

1 A policeman
2 a Yes, at NK and Gallerian; **b** They want a cup of coffee; **c** Nordiska museet, Vasamuseet, Skansen; **d** Vasa, a warship from 1628
3 a – 2; **b** – 3; **c** – 1
4 a Gå over Vasagatan; **b** Vandra vidare längs Klarabergsgatan; **c** Gå längs Hamngatan.

Practice

1 b Jag svänger in på den sjätte gatan härifrån; **c** Eva bor i det tredje huset härifrån; **d** Den trettonde i fjärde; **e** Den elfte i elfte.
2 a Tala om hur vi kommer till Skansen!; **b** Fortsätt sedan rakt fram till Strandvägen!; **c** Gå härifrån till Sergels Torg!; **d** Fråga damen där borta om resten av vägen!; **e** Vandra nu vidare till Vasamuseet!
3 a I drive on the street; **b** Don't crash into the car over there; **c** We visit Aunt Emma every day; **d** We say hello or how do you do when greeting someone.

Speaking

Turisterna: Hur kommer vi till Skansen härifrån?
Polisen: Det är bäst att gå härifrån till Sergels Torg
Turisterna: Är det bara rakt fram?
Polisen: Ja, gå tvärs över Vasagatan och fortsätt längs Klarabergsgatan
Turisterna: Tack, det klarar vi nog
Polisen: Lycka till, ha en bra dag!

Pronunciation

a Den tjugoförsta i sjätte; **b** Den tjugofjärde i tolfte; **c** Den trettioförsta i tolfte

Conversation 2

1 ta, kör, sakta ner, stanna, visa, fyll, låt
2 a Stanna och visa tecken!; **b** Jag vill inte ha fortkörningsböter; **c** Kör inte för fort! Sakta ner!

Reading

1 1 –d, **2** – g, **3** – f, **4** – j, **5** – k, **6** – l, **7** – c, **8** – e, **9** – h, **10** – b, **11** – a, **12** – i
2 a – 1, **b** – 5, **c** – 11, **d** – 7, **e** – 9, **f** – 10, **g** – 4, **h** – 3, **i** – 6, **j** – 2, **k** – 12, **l** – 8

Test yourself

1 a Övergångsstället, längs; **b** Tror, en kaffepaus; **c** Vattnet, bron; **d** Säkerhetsbältet, fort
2 a Vart ska jag köra i rondellen?; **b** Vi är/bor på tredje våningen; **c** Fortsätt rakt fram, du är snart där; **d** Du kör riktigt bra.

R2 (UNITS 4–6)

1 Kaféer, stockholmare, koppar, böcker, tidningar, språk, musiker, stolarna
2 a Lennart är den yngste av bröderna, hans bröder är mycket äldre; **b** Kebnekaise är det högsta berget/fjället i Sverige, men mycket lägre än Mont Blanc; **c** Göteborg är mindre än Stockholm men större än Malmö; **d** I oktober är vädret sämre än i juli men bättre än i februari.
3 a Halv åtta på morgonen; **b** Tjugo över elva på förmiddagen; **c** Kvart över tre på eftermiddagen; **d** Fem i halv tolv på kvällen/natten
4 a Skriv ditt namn här!; **b** Se upp när det kommer en bil!; **c** Sväng till höger i rondellen!; **d** Tryck din kod i uttagsautomaten!
5 a I drive on the street; **b** I crash into the tree; **c** I greet him when I see him in the street; **d** I visit my aunt in Lund when I am in Sweden.

6 a När föddes August Strindberg, och när dog han?; **b** Var bodde han/ I vilka städer bodde han?; **c** Hur skrev han sina manuskript?; **d** Varför träffade han sina vänner i Lund den 22 januari 1899?
7 a Tjugonionde februari; **b** Fjortonde juli; **c** Trettionde november; **d** Trettonde december
8 a Söderut; **b** Österut; **c** Norrut; **d** Västerut
9 a Greta and Barbro are sisters-in-law; **b** They want to buy gifts for their grandchildren; **c** Greta buys a big puzzle for her daughter's daughters; **d** Barbro buys two books for her daughter's sons; **e** They have coffee at a cafe **f** They take the bus home.
10 a Den populära expediten talar flera språk: engelska, tyska, franska och spanska; **b** Han provar de största bruna skorna i affären; **c** Hon gillar de röda hattarna, de svarta klänningarna, och de unga männen; **d** De tar ut pengar från uttagsautomaten och flyger till Kina; **e** Vi köper äpplen, vita ljus och en röd dalahäst.

UNIT 7

Eating in Sweden

Coffee, milk, rusks, bread, butter, cheese, honey, jam, eggs

Vocabulary builder

Knife, main course, well done

Conversation 1

1 For her starter Ebba chooses a shrimp cocktail and for her main course sole; Sven has salmon on toast and fillet steak, and as dessert they both have chocolate mousse.
2 a A table by the window; **b** Well done; **c** Bright red tulips; **d** Spring

Language discovery

Här är fönsterbordet som ni bokade

Practice

1 Bokade, önskade, började, hade, funderade, verkade, trodde, avslutade; Kom, kunde, blev, fick, fanns, tog, var, lät, ville, föreslog
2 I came to Gothenburg yesterday. She couldn't come. Ebba was happy when she got the flowers. Salmon was not on the menu. She chose fish and he chose meat. The music was too loud, it sounded horrible. He wanted fillet steak, and she wanted sole. Emma suggested chocolate mousse.

3 a Flickan som sitter vid bordet är min syster; **b** Maten som vi äter är mycket god; **c** De tre vännerna som åt lunch på IKEA är kolleger.

Speaking

Ebba: Nu ska vi se vad som finns på matsedeln
Kyparen: Dagens special är rödspätta och oxfilé
Sven: Jag tror jag tar en kötträtt
Kyparen: Ska den vara lättstekt, medium eller välstekt?
Sven: Välstekt, tack. Och sedan chokladmousse för oss båda.
Kyparen: Och vill ni avsluta med en kopp kaffe?

Conversation 2

1 Meatballs with brown gravy, potatoes and lingonberries; salmon; soup; coffee, cinnamon bun and almond cake
2 a She will have a proper meal when she gets home; **b** Soup, bread, a drink; **c** She has chosen soup for lunch.

Reading

a Flour, milk, egg; **b** Fried on both sides; **c** Lingonberry or strawberry jam; **d** Melted butter has already been poured into the batter

Test yourself

1 a Ebba fyller år i dag; **b** Sven bjuder henne på middag ute; **c** Per, David och Sanna går till IKEA; **d** De äter lunch på restaurangen där; **e** Per gillar husmanskosten; **f** Sanna tar fel bestick.
2 a – 6; **b** – 8; **c** – 9; **d** – 7; **e** – 10; **f** – 1; **g** – 4; **h** – 2 ; **i** – 3; **j** – 5
3 a Musiken var för hög, det lät förskräckligt; **b** Knallröda tulpaner är mina favoritblommor; **c** Jag tar köttbullar. Jag gillar husmanskost; **d** Häll lagom mycket smet i stekpannan, stek pannkakan på ena sidan, vänd den sedan.

UNIT 8

Swedes at home

Matta, fönsterbräda, vägg, svensk, gardin, möbel, krukväxt

Vocabulary builder

Guest room, nursery, bathroom, microwave, freezer, washing machine

Conversation 1

1 They are shown the hall, the guestroom, the living room and its dining corner, the kitchen, the study, the nursery, the master bedroom, the laundry and the sauna.
2 a A stove with a grill, a dishwasher, a microwave, a large fridge and freezer; **b** A desk, bookcases, a television; **c** On the terrace; **d** The sauna
3 a – 2; **b** – 3; **c** – 1
4 a Känn er som hemma; **b** Det är härligt med bastu innan man lägger sig.

Practice

1 a Han slog sig men lugnade ner sig; **b** Jag såg att hon hade kammat sig.
2 a Vi ska äta middag på terrassen; **b** Han hade sett en älg i trädgården.
3 a Katten ligger i sängen; **b** Hon har lagt den där; **c** Han satte sig i soffan; **d** Nu sitter han där.

Conversation 2

a She has seen a lot, got to know many Swedes and been in the sauna and the lake; **b** She has stayed at home, read crime stories, been in the water and seen her mother.

Speaking

Bonnie: Hej Mary, välkommen tillbaka,. Var har du varit i sommar?
Mary: Vi har varit i Sverige.
Bonnie: Kul. Vad har ni hittat på?
Mary: Vi har sett mycket av Sverige och lärt känna många svenskar. Vad har du gjort?
Bonnie: Jag har varit hemma och läst deckare.
Mary: Har du hunnit resa?
Bonnie: Jag har hälsat på min mamma som flyttat till min syster.
Mary: Så bra att hon bestämt sig.

Test yourself

1 -are
2 a – 4; **b** – 6; **c** – 7; **d** – 2; **e** – 8; **f** – 5; **g** – 1; **h** – 3
3 a She sits down on the sofa; **b** She lies down on the carpet; **c** They wash before dinner; **d** He sat on the sofa; **e** He lay on the carpet; **f** They washed before they had dinner.

UNIT 9

Sport

High jump; long jump; bike race; ski race

Vocabulary builder
Tennis court, book club, go to the gym

Conversation 1
1 Tennis, golf, riding, soccer, slalom, ice hockey, gymnastics, handball, chess
2 a He watched the Båstad tennis games; **b** He took them to the riding school; **c** She reads a book; **d** They discuss books and current films.

Practice
1 b otroligt; **c** fantastiskt; **d** väldigt; **e** kolossalt
2 a obekväm; **b** otrevlig; **c** ointressant; **d** ogärna; **e** ogilla

Conversation 2
1 Karin likes documentaries; Britta doesn't. They are both interested in music.
2 a They make her happy; **b** Songs about the spring; **c** They practise once a week; **d** She played the piano
3 väldigt, otroligt, kolossalt, fantastiskt

Listening
a Warm weather with temperature above 25 degrees, risk of thunder; **b** Unstable cloudy weather, cooler winds; **c** Rain coming in from the northwest

Reading
a Zlatan scored all the evening's goals; b The first goal came after a pass from Henke Larsson; c The fourth goal came one minute before full time, on a penalty; d The British goalkeeper stood no chance

Reading
a He will celebrate that it's 50 years since he got his doctorate; **b** His daughter-in-law and three hitchhikers; **c** It is summer; **d** Ingmar Bergman directed the film, Victor Sjöström played the main character

Test yourself

3 a – 3; **b** – 6; **c** – 5; **d** – 1; **e** – 2; **f** – 4

UNIT 10

Swedish holidays

Leap year, leap day

Conversation 1

1 They light candles, stay indoors out of the cold, drink mulled wine and observe the traditions.

2 a inomhus, utomhus; **b** på; **c** till; **d** av, i; **e** med, i, under; **f** genom/längs; **g** i, på

Practice

1 a under, under; **b** genom; **c** för en time sedan; **d** i somras; **e** köptes; **f** tänds; **g** de där; **h** det här

Conversation 2

Summer celebrations: Midsummer; crayfish parties; winter celebrations: the Nobel Day festivities, Lucia, Christmas

Speaking

Carl: Vilken helg är din favorit?

Karin: Jag gillar påsken eftersom jag gillar ägg, både hönsägg och chokladägg.

Carl: Midsommar är min favorithelg och ett sommarbröllop på midsommarafton är romantiskt.

Karin: Absolut. Kräftfesterna i augusti är också en av sommarens höjdpunkter.

Carl: På allhelgonadaghen tänder vi ljus på gravarna.

Karin: Och sedan längtar vi efter de långa ljusa sommarnätterna!

Reading 2

1 a Dynamite; **b** Five in Stockholm, one in Oslo; **c** The economics prize; **d** Alfred Nobel died on 10 December

Writing

a Vilken är din favoritmånad?; **b** När är påsken?; **c** Varför tänder vi ljus på gravarna?; **d** Vem firar vi den 13 december?

Test yourself

1 Skärtorsdag, långfredag, påskafton, påskdagen, annandag påsk
2 Jultomten. 24 December.
3 Kemipriset, fysikpriset, medicinpriset, litteraturpriset, fredspriset
4 Ekonomipriset till Alfred Nobels minne.

R3 (UNITS 7–10)

1 a Ebba gets red tulips from Sven on her birthday; **b** Per had meatballs and potatoes for lunch yesterday; **c** Zlatan scored three goals in the match and the Danish goalkeeper had no chance; **d** The translator knew five languages, the interpreter knew seven; **e** The book that was lying on the table was put up on the shelf by the librarian; **f** The journalist wrote in the newspaper about the town that was spared in the earthquake.
2 a – 5; **b** – 3; **c** – 1; **d** – 6; **e** – 2; **f** – 4
3 Såg – har sett – ska se; Handlar – har handlat – ska handla; Besöker – besökte – ska besöka; Åt – har ätit – ska äta; Hälsar – hälsade – har hälsat; Köpte – har köpt – ska köpa; Går – har gått – ska gå
4 a Annika gick på bio, Johan spelade fotboll; **b** Han tränar varje vecka, på lördagen; **c** Ja, både Erik, Kalle, Mats och Jens är intresserade av sport; **d** Han läser många böcker; **e** Annika gillar att läsa deckare och promenera; **f** Ja, det finns fina golfbanor och golfklubbar; **g** Johans fru kommer från Frankrike; **h** De reser gärna till Norge; **i** Hon badar och går på konstmuseer.
5 They start the meal with a little soup. **a** De äter soppa; **b** Hon ber om receptet; **c** Han har läst nya kurser i ekonomi; **d** Hon är lärare; **e** Hon ska träffa kompisar; **f** Det är trist att läsa ekonomi; **g** De äter en chockladmousse som Annika lagat; **h** De sätter sig i soffan och diskuterar vad de ska göra vecka 46.
6 a That they have their big Christmas dinner at a restaurant; **b** Then they can have a slimmed down version at home; **c** Ham and red cabbage; **d** The various pickled herring dishes; **e** It is a very popular restaurant

Swedish–English glossary

-0 indicates that the singular and plural forms of the noun are identical.

adjö	*goodbye*
adventsljus (-et -0)	*advent candle*
affär (-en -er)	*shop*
aktuell	*up to date, topical*
akvarellmålning (-en -ar)	*watercolour*
aldrig	*never*
alldeles	*quite, exactly*
allihop	*all, everybody*
alltid	*always*
andra	*others*
anländ/a (-er -e anlänt)	*arrive*
anpass/a sig (-ar -ade -at)	*adjust*
anteckn/a (-ar -ade -at)	*note down*
använd/a (-er -e använt)	*use*
arbet/a (-ar -ade -at)	*work*
avslut/a (-ar -ade -at)	*finish*
bad/a (-ar -ade -at)	*bathe, swim*
bara	*only*
barn (-et -0)	*child*
barnkammare (-en -0)	*nursery*
barnpassning (-en)	*child care*
barnvakt (-en -er)	*babysitter*
bastu (-n -r)	*sauna*
be (-r bad bett)	*pray, beg*
behöv/a (-er -de -t)	*need*
bekväm	*comfortable*
bensin (-en)	*petrol*
bero på (-r -dde -tt)	*depend on*
berömd	*famous*
besök (-et -0)	*visit*
bestäm/ma (-er -de-t)	*decide*
bestick (-et -0)	*cutlery*
betal/a (-ar -ade -at)	*pay*
bibliotek (-et -0)	*library*
bil (-en -ar)	*car*
biljett (-en -er)	*ticket*
biluthyrare (-n -0)	*car hire agent*
bit/a (-er bet bitit)	*bite*
bli (-r blev blivit)	*become*
blomma (-n -or)	*flower*
blöt	*wet*
bo (-r -dde -tt)	*live, inhabit*
bok/a (-ar -ade -at)	*book*
bokhyll/a (-an -or)	*bookcase*
bord (-et -0)	*table*
bra	*good, well*
brick/a (-n -or)	*tray*
bro (- n -ar)	*bridge*
bröllop (-et -0)	*wedding*
bruk/a (-ar -ade -at)	*usually do*

burk (-en -ar)	*jar, tin*
byt/a (-er -te -t)	*change, exchange*
bytesrätt	*money back guarantee*
byx/a (- n -or)	*trousers*
börj/a (-ar -ade -at)	*begin*
dag (-en -ar)	*day*
dagis (-et -0)	*nursery*
dataspel (-et -0)	*computer game*
deckare (-n -0)	*detective; crime story*
del/a (-ar -de -t) ut	*hand out, distribute*
delvis	*partly*
dessvärre	*unfortunately*
disk (-en -ar)	*counter*
disk/a (-ar -ade -at)	*wash up*
diskmaskin (-en -er)	*dishwasher*
doft (-en -er)	*fragrance*
drick/a (-er drack druckit)	*drink*
dusch (-en -ar)	*shower*
då	*then*
dålig (sämre sämst)	*bad, ill*
därifrån	*from there*
dö (-r dog dött)	*die*
efterrätt (-en -er)	*dessert*
eftersom	*while, because*
ensam	*alone, lonely*
erbjud/a (-er erbjöd erbjudit)	*offer*
faktiskt	*actually, as a matter of fact*
fest (-en -er)	*party*
fir/a (-ar -ade -at)	*celebrate*
fisk (-en -ar)	*fish*
flyg/a (-er flög flugit)	*fly*
flygplan (-et -0)	*aeroplane*
flytt/a (-ar -ade -at)	*move*
fortfarande	*still*
fortsätt/a (-er -satte -satt)	*continue*
fotgängare (-n -0)	*pedestrian*
fråg/a (-an -or)	*question*
fram	*forward*
framme	*get there*
fred (-en)	*peace*
frukost (-en -ar)	*breakfast*
fruntim/mer (-ret -0)	*woman*
frys (-en -ar)	*freezer*
från	*from*
funger/a (-ar -ade -at)	*function*
fyll/a (-er -de -t) i	*fill in*
fylla år	*have one´s birthday*
fysik (-en)	*physics*
färg (-en -er)	*colour, paint*
färj/a (-an -or)	*ferry*
födelsedag (-en -ar)	*birthday*
följ/a (-er -de -t)	*follow*

fönst/er (-ret -0)	*window*
förbjuden	*forbidden, prohibited*
förenkl/a (-ar -ade -at)	*simplify*
föreslå (-r föreslog föreslagit)	*suggest*
förlåt	*I am sorry*
förmögenhet (-en -er)	*wealth*
förrätt (-en -er)	*starter*
förslag (-et -0)	*suggestion*
gaff/el (-eln -lar)	*fork*
gat/a (-an -or)	*street*
gill/a (-ar -ade -at)	*like*
glass (-en)	*ice cream*
glögg (-en)	*mulled wine*
glöm/ma (-mer -de -t)	*forget*
grad (-en -er)	*degree*
gran (-en -ar)	*Christmas tree, spruce*
gymnastik (-en)	*physical education, gymnastics*
gå (-r gick gått)	*go, walk*
gård (-en -ar)	*courtyard; farm*
gärna	*gladly, willingly*
gäst (-en -er)	*guest*
gör/a (göra gjorde gjort)	*do*
ha (-r hade haft)	*have*
hallon (-et -0)	*raspberry*
handl/a (-ar -ade -at)	*buy*
hedr/a (-ar -ade -at)	*honour*
helg (-en -er)	*holiday*
helgon (-et -0)	*saint*
helt enkelt	*quite simply*
hemväg (-en -ar)	*way home*
het/a (-er -tte -at)	*be called*
hinn/a (-er hann hunnit)	*have time*
hiss (-en -ar)	*elevator, lift*
hitt/a (-ar -ade -at)	*find*
hjälp (-en)	*help*
hjält/e (-en -ar)	*hero*
hopp/a (-ar -ade -at)	*jump*
hopp/as (-as -ades -ats)	*hope for*
hovmästar/e (-en -0)	*head waiter, maître d'hôtel*
hund (-en -ar)	*dog*
hurra	*hurrah, hooray!*
husmanskost (-en)	*traditional basic food*
huvudrätt (-en -er)	*main course*
hyr/a (-0 -de -t)	*rent*
häftig	*cool*
häls/a (-ar -ade -at)	*greet*
hämt/a (-ar -ade -at)	*fetch*
här	*here*
härifrån	*from here*
härlig	*glorious, splendid*
höger	*right*

högsäsong (-en -er) *high season*
höjdpunkt (-en -er) *highlight*
hön/a (-an -or) *hen*
hörn/a (-an -or) *corner*
höst (-en -ar) *autumn, fall*
icke-rökare (-n -0) *non-smoker*
igen *again*
inaktuell *outdated*
industriman (-nen -män) *industrialist*
ingenjör (-en -er) *engineer*
innan *before*
inne, inomhus *inside, indoors*
instift/a (-ar -ade -at) *establish*
inte alls *not at all*
ja, javisst *yes, yes of course*
jobb/a (-ar -ade -at) *work*
jordgubb/e (-en -ar) *strawberry*
julgran (-en -ar) *Christmas tree*
julotta (-n -or) *church service very early on Christmas Day*
jättebra *super!*
kaffe (-t) *coffee*
kall *cold*
kanelbull/e (-en -ar) *cinnamon bun*
kanske *maybe*
kapp/a (-an -or) *coat*
kemi *chemistry*
klack (-en -ar) *heel*
kläder (-na) *clothes*
klänning (-en -ar) *dress*
klar/a (-ar -ade -at) *fix*
knallröd *bright red*
kniv (-en -ar) *knife*
knyt/a (-er knöt knutit) *tie a knot*
koll/a (-ar -ade -at) *check*
komm/a (-er kom kommit) *come*
kompis (-en -ar) *mate, pal*
kontant *cash*
kontroller/a (-ar -ade -at) *control*
kors/a (-ar -ade -at) *cross*
kort (-et -0) *card*
kost/a (-ar -de -t) *cost*
kräft/a (-an -or) *crayfish*
krig (-et -0) *war*
kul *fun*
kunna (kan kunde kunnat) *know*
kvarter (-et -0) *city block*
kvinn/a (-an -or) *woman*
kvitto (-t -n) *receipt*
kväll (-en -ar) *evening*
kylig *chilly*
kylskåp (-et -0) *fridge*
käk/a (-ar -ade -at) *eat*
källar/e (-en -0) *cellar, basement*

känn/a (-er kände känt)	*know*
kök (-et -0)	*kitchen*
köp/a (-er -te -t)	*buy*
kör/a (kör -de -t)	*drive*
körkort (-et -0)	*driving licence*
körsång (-en)	*choir singing*
kött (-et)	*meat*
lag/a (-ar -ade -at)	*cook*
lagom	*just right*
lax (-en -ar)	*salmon*
lejon (-et -0)	*lion*
lektion (-en -er)	*lesson*
lingon (-et -0)	*lingonberry*
lite	*little*
ljus	*light, fair*
ljus (-et -0)	*candle, light*
lov (-et, -0)	*holiday*
lov/a (-ar -ade -at)	*promise*
låt/a (-er lät låtit)	*let*
lägg/a (-er lade lagt)	*lay down, put down*
lämn/a (-ar-ade -at)	*leave*
länge	*long, a long time*
längs	*along*
längt/a (-ar -ade -at) efter	*long for*
lär/a (lär -de -t) känna	*get to know*
lätt	*light, easy*
mandelkak/a (-an -or)	*almond cake*
mathörn/a (-an -or)	*dining corner*
matsedel (-n -sedlar)	*menu*
med	*with*
meny (-n -er)	*menu*
mer	*more*
middag (-en -ar)	*dinner*
midnattsmäss/a (-n -or)	*midnight mass*
minnas (minns mindes)	*remember*
mjöl (-et)	*flour*
mjölk (-en)	*milk*
morgon (-en morgnar)	*morning*
mycket	*very, much*
må (-r -dde -tt)	*feel, be*
måste	*must*
mätt	*full, satisfied*
mörker (mörkret)	*darkness*
namn (-et -0)	*name*
natt (-en nätter)	*night*
naturligtvis	*naturally, of course*
nej	*no*
nervös	*nervous*
nog	*enough; probably*
nuförtiden	*nowadays*
nyckel (-n nycklar)	*key*
nöjd	*satisfied*
nära	*near, close*
nästa	*next*
och	*and*

också	*also, too*
oftast	*most often*
omtyckt	*well liked*
omväxling (-en)	*variety, variation*
ordn/a (-ar -ade -at)	*organize*
otäck	*horrible*
ovanlig	*unusual*
oxfilé (-n -er)	*fillet steak*
parker/a (-ar -ade -at)	*park*
pass(-et -0)	*passport*
pengar	*money*
pingstafton (-en -aftnar)	*Whitsun evening*
plan (-en -er)	*plan*
planer/a (-ar -ade -at)	*plan*
plats (-en -er)	*place*
plock/a (-ar -ade -at) fram	*take out*
potatis (-en -ar)	*potato*
precis	*precisely, exactly*
prick (-en -ar)	*dot*
pris (-et -er)	*price*
promener/a (-ar -ade -at)	*walk, stroll*
prov/a, pröv/a (-ar -ade -at)	*try, test*
påhälsning (-en -ar)	*visit*
påsk (-en -ar)	*Easter*
rabatt (-en -er)	*discount*
rakt fram	*straight ahead*
reception (-en -er)	*front desk*
regn (-et -0)	*rain*
res/a (-er -te -t)	*travel*
respektlös	*disrespectful*
restaurangvagn (-en -ar)	*dining car*
returrätt (-en -er)	*money back guarantee*
rid/a (-er red ridit)	*ride*
riksbank (-en -er)	*national bank*
riktigt	*right, correct*
roligt	*funny*
rondell (-en -er)	*roundabout*
rum (-met -0)	*room*
rund/a (-ar -ade -at)	*drive around*
råd (-et -0)	*advice*
räk/a (-an -or)	*shrimp*
rödspätt/a (-an -or)	*flounder*
rökförbud (-et -0)	*smoking ban*
sakt/a (-ar -ade -at) ner	*slow down*
samma	*same*
sats/a (-ar -ade -at)	*bet*
schack (-et)	*chess*
schem/a (-at -an)	*timetable*
se (ser såg sett)	*see*
sedan	*then, later*
semest/er (-ern -rar)	*holiday*
sen	*late*
server/a (-ar -ade -at)	*serve*
sill (-en -ar)	*herring*
sista	*last*

sitt/a (-er satt suttit)	*sit*
sjung/a (-er sjöng sjungit)	*sing*
självklart	*self-evident, obvious*
sjö (-n -ar)	*lake*
ska (skulle)	*shall, will*
skaff/a (-ar -ade -at)	*provide, get*
skaplig	*fair enough, quite ok*
sked (-en -ar)	*spoon*
skepp (-et -0)	*ship*
skid/a (-an -or)	*ski*
skinn (-et -0)	*skin*
sko (-n -r)	*shoe*
skoj	*fun*
skottdag (-en -ar)	*leap day*
skönt	*pleasant*
skriv/a (-er skrev skrivit)	*write*
skylt (-en -ar)	*sign*
slipp/a (-er slapp sluppit)	*escape, be spared*
slå (-r slog slagit)	*beat, win over*
smak (-en -er)	*taste*
smaklig	*tasty*
smet (-en)	*batter*
smyg/a (-er smög smugit)	*slip, sneak*
smält/a (-er -e -t)	*melt*
snabb	*fast*
snart	*soon*
snäll	*kind*
snö (-n)	*snow*
sommar (-en somrar)	*summer*
sopp/a (-an -or)	*soup*
sov/a (-er sov sovit)	*sleep*
sovvagn (-en -ar)	*sleeper*
spis (-en -ar)	*oven, stove, fireplace*
spännande	*thrilling*
stad (-en städer)	*town, city*
stann/a (-ar -ade -at)	*stop*
stek/a (-er -te -t)	*fry*
storlek (-en -ar)	*size*
strax	*soon*
strålande	*glorious*
stövel (-n stövlar)	*boots*
svår	*difficult*
sväng/a (-er -de -t) in	*turn into*
sylt (-en)	*jam*
så	*so*
sådan	*such*
säker	*safe, secure*
säkerhetsbält/e (-et -en)	*seatbelt*
ta (-r tog tagit)	*take*
tack	*thanks*
tambur (-en -er)	*hall*
tank/a (-ar -ade -at)	*fill the tank*
teck/en (-net -0)	*sign*
tennisban/a (-an -or)	*tennis court*
tesked (-en -ar)	*teaspoon*
tid (-en -er)	*time*
tidig	*early*

tidtabell (-en -er)	*timetable*
till dess	*until then*
till minne av	*in memory of*
till, tills	*to, until*
tillbaka	*back*
titt/a (-ar -ade -at) in	*come by*
tjena, tjenare	*hi*
tokig i	*mad about*
torg (-et -0)	*market, square*
torktumlare (-n -0)	*tumble dryer*
träd (-et -0)	*tree*
trädgård (-en -ar)	*garden*
tränare (-n -0)	*trainer, coach*
trängselskatt (-en -er)	*congestion charge*
trevlig	*nice*
trist	*gloomy, sad*
troligen	*probably*
tröj/a (-an -or)	*sweater*
tulpan (-en -er)	*tulip*
tur (-en)	*turn; luck*
tur/as (-0 -ades -ats) om	*take turns*
tvärs over	*straight across*
tvättstug/a (-an -or)	*laundry*
tyck/a (-er -te -t) om	*think; like*
tyvärr	*unfortunately*
tåg (-et -0)	*train*
tänk/a (-er -te -t) på	*think of*
ugn (-en -ar)	*oven*
uppfinnare (-n -0)	*inventor*
uppgift (-en -er)	*task*
upplös/a (-er -te -t)	*dissolve*
ursäkt/a (-ar -ade -at)	*apologies, I am sorry*
utantill	*by heart*
utdelning (-en-ar)	*distribution, delivery*
ute	*outside*
utforsk/a (-ar -ade -at)	*explore*
utmärkt	*excellent*
utomhus	*outside (the house)*
utsikt (-en -er)	*view*
vandr/a (-ar -ade -at)	*walk, wander*
vanlig	*common*
var sin	*one each*
vardag (-en -ar)	*weekday, every day*
varsågod	*please*
våt	*wet*
veck/a (-an -or)	*week*
verk/a (-ar -ade -at)	*seem*
verkligen	*really, certainly*
vidare	*further*
vint/er (-ern -rar)	*winter*
vis/a (-ar -ade -at)	*show*
visitkort (-et -0)	*business card*
vispgrädde (-n)	*whipped cream*
vistelse (-n -r)	*stay*
vuxen (vuxna)	*adult*

våning (-en -ar)	*apartment, flat*	årlig	*annual*
vår (-en -ar)	*spring*	årstid (-en -er)	*season*
väd/er (-ret väder)	*weather*	ägg (-et -0)	*egg*
väg (-en -ar)	*way, road*	äktenskap (-et -0)	*marriage*
väl	*good, well*	älska (-r -de -t)	*love*
välj/a (-er valde valt)	*choose*	äntligen	*finally, at last*
välkommen	*welcome*	ärtsopp/a (-an -or)	*pea soup*
vänster	*left*	ät/a (-er åt ätit)	*eat*
vänt/a (-ar -ade -at)	*wait*	även	*also*
värld (-en -ar)	*world*	öv/a (-ar -ade -at)	*practice*
väsk/a (-an -or)	*suitcase*	över	*over, above*
åk/a (-er -te -t)	*go, travel*	övergångsställ/e (-et -en)	*pedestrian crossing*
år (-et -0)	*year*	övning (-en -ar)	*practice*

English–Swedish glossary

actually, as a matter of fact	faktiskt
adjust	anpass/a sig (-ar -ade -at)
adult	vuxen (vuxna)
advent candle	adventsljus (-et -0)
advice	råd (-et -0)
again	igen
airplane	flygplan (-et -0)
all, everybody	allihop
almond cake	mandelkak/a (-an -or)
alone, lonely	ensam
along	längs
also	även
also, too	också
always	alltid
and	och
annual	årlig
apartment, flat	våning (-en -ar)
apologies, I am sorry	ursäkt/a (-ar -ade -at)
arrive	anländ/a (-er -e anlänt)
autumn, fall	höst (-en -ar)
babysitter	barnvakt (-en -er)
back	tillbaka
bad, ill	dålig (sämre sämst)
bathe	bad/a (-ar -ade -at)
batter	smet (-en)
be called	het/a (-er -tte -at)
beat, win over	slå (-r slog slagit)
become	bli (-r blev blivit)
before	innan
begin	börj/a (-ar -ade -at)
bet	sats/a (-ar -ade -at)
birthday	födelsedag (-en -ar)
bite	bit/a (-er bet bitit)
book	bok/a (-ar -ade -at)
bookcase	bokhyll/a (-an -or)
boots	stövel (-n stövlar)
breakfast	frukost (-en -ar)
bridge	bro (- n -ar)
bright red	knallröd
business card	visitkort (-et -0)
buy	handl/a (-ar -ade -at)
buy	köp/a (-er -te -t)
by heart	utantill
candle, light	ljus (-et -0)
car	bil (-en -ar)
car hire agent	biluthyrare (-n -0)

card	kort (-et -0)
cash	kontant
celebrate	fir/a (-ar -ade -at)
cellar, basement	källar/e (-en -0)
change, exchange	byt/a (-er -te -t)
check	koll/a (-ar -ade -at)
check-in desk	reception (-en -er)
chemistry	kemi
chess	schack (-et)
child	barn (-et -0)
child care	barnpassning (-en)
chilly	kylig
choir singing	körsång (-en)
choose	välj/a (-er valde valt)
Christmas tree	julgran (-en -ar)
church service very early on Christmas Day	julotta (-n -or)
Christmas tree, spruce	gran (-en -ar)
cinnamon bun	kanelbull/e (-en -ar)
city block	kvarter (-et -0)
clothes	kläder (-na)
coat	kapp/a (-an -or)
coach, trainer	tränare (-n -0)
coffee	kaffe (-t)
cold	kall
colour, paint	färg (-en -er)
come	komm/a (-er kom kommit)
come by	titt/a (-ar -ade -at) in
comfortable	bekväm
common	vanlig
computer game	dataspel (-et -0)
congestion charge	trängselskatt (-en -er)
continue	fortsätt/a (-er -satte -satt)
control	kontroller/a (ar -ade -at)
cook	lag/a (-ar -ade -at)
cool	häftig
corner	hörn/a (-an -or)
cost	kost/a (-ar -de -t)
counter	disk (-en -ar)
courtyard, farm	gård (-en -ar)
crayfish	kräft/a (-an -or)
cross	kors/a (-ar -ade -at)
cutlery	bestick (-et -0)
darkness	mörker (mörkret)
day	dag (-en -ar)
decide	bestäm/ma (-er -de-t)
degree	grad (-en -er)
depend on	bero på (-r -dde -tt)
dessert	efterrätt (-en -er)
detective; crime story	deckare (-n -0)

die	dö (-r dog dött)
difficult	svår
dining corner	mathörn/a (-an -or)
dinner	middag (-en -ar)
dining car	restaurangvagn (-en -ar)
discount	rabatt (-en -er)
dishwasher	diskmaskin (-en -er)
disrespectful	respektlös
dissolve	upplös/a (-er -te -t)
distribution, delivery	utdelning (-en-ar)
do	gör/a (gör gjorde gjort)
dog	hund (-en -ar)
dot	prick (-en -ar)
dress	klänning (-en -ar)
drink	drick/a (-er drack druckit)
drive	kör/a (kör -de -t)
drive around	rund/a (-ar -ade-at)
driving licence	körkort (-et -0)
early	tidig
Easter	påsk (-en -ar)
eat	käk/a (-ar -ade -at)
eat	ät/a (-er åt ätit)
egg	ägg (-et -0)
elevator, lift	hiss (-en -ar)
engineer	ingenjör (-en -er)
enough, probably	nog
escape, be spared	slipp/a (-er slapp sluppit)
establish	instift/a (-ar -ade -at)
evening	kväll (-en -ar)
excellent	utmärkt
explore	utforsk/a (-ar -ade -at)
fair enough, quite ok	skaplig
famous	berömd
fast	snabb
feel, be	må (-r -dde -tt)
ferry	färj/a (-an -or)
fetch	hämt/a (-ar -ade -at)
fill in	fyll/a (-er -de -t) i
fillet steak	oxfilé (-n -er)
fill the tank	tank/a (-ar -ade -at)
finally, at last	äntligen
find	hitt/a (-ar -ade -at)
finish	avslut/a (-ar -ade -at)
fish	fisk (-en -ar, -0)
fix	klar/a (-ar -ade -at)
flounder	rödspätt/a (-an -or)
flour	mjöl (-et)
flower	blomma (-n -or)
fly	flyg/a (-er flög flugit)
follow	följ/a (-er -de -t)
forbidden, prohibited	förbjuden

forget	glöm/ma (-mer -de -t)
fork	gaff/el (-eln -lar)
forward	fram
fragrance	doft (-en -er)
freezer	frys (-en -ar)
fridge	kylskåp (-et -0)
from	från
from here	härifrån
from there	därifrån
fry	stek/a (-er -te -t)
full, satisfied	mätt
fun	kul, skoj
function	funger/a (-ar -ade -at)
funny	roligt
further	vidare
garden	trädgård (-en -ar)
get there	framme
get to know	lär/a (-0 -de -t) känna
gladly, willingly	gärna
gloomy, sad	trist
glorious	strålande, härlig
go, travel	åk/a (-er -te -t)
go, walk	gå (-r gick gått)
good, well	bra, väl
goodbye	adjö
greet	häls/a (-ar -ade -at)
guest	gäst (-en -er)
hall	tambur (-en -er)
hand out, distribute	del/a (-ar -de -t) ut
have	ha (-r hade haft)
have one's birthday	fylla år
have time	hinn/a (-er hann hunnit)
head waiter, maître d'hôtel	hovmästar/e (-en -0)
heel	klack (-en -ar)
help	hjälp (-en)
hen	hön/a (-an -or)
here	här
hero	hjält/e (-en -ar)
herring	sill (-en -ar)
hi	tjena, tjenare
high season	högsäsong (-en -er)
highlight	höjdpunkt (-en -er)
holiday	helg (-en -er), lov (-et, -0), semest/er (-ern -rar)
honour	hedr/a (-ar -ade -at)
hope for	hopp/as (-as -ades -ats)
horrible	otäck
hurrah, hooray!	hurra
ice cream	glass (-en)
in memory of	till minne av
industrialist	industriman (-nen -män)

inside, indoors	inne, inomhus
inventor	uppfinnare (-n -0)
jam	sylt (-en)
jar, tin	burk (-en -ar)
jump	hopp/a (-ar -ade -at)
just right	lagom
key	nyckel (-n nycklar)
kind	snäll
kitchen	kök (-et -0)
knife	kniv (-en -ar)
know	kunna (kan kunde kunnat), känn/a (-er kände känt)
lake	sjö (-n -ar)
last	sista
late	sen
laundry	tvättstug/a (-an -or)
lay down, put down	lägg/a (-er lade lagt)
leap day	skottdag (-en -ar)
leave	lämn/a (-ar-ade -at)
left	vänster
lesson	lektion (-en -er)
let	låt/a (-er lät låtit)
library	bibliotek (-et -0)
light, easy	lätt
light, fair	ljus
like	gill/a (-ar -ade -at)
lingonberry	lingon (-et -0)
lion	lejon (-et -0)
little	lite
live, inhabit	bo (-r -dde -tt)
long for	längt/a (-ar -ade -at efter)
long, a long time	länge
love	älska (-r -de -t)
mad about	tokig i
main course	huvudrätt (-en -er)
market, square	torg (-et -0)
marriage	äktenskap (-et -0)
mate, pal	kompis (-en -ar)
maybe	kanske
meat	kött (-et)
melt	smält/a (-er -e -t)
menu	matsedel (-n -sedlar), meny (-n -er)
midnight mass	midnattsmäss/a (-n -or)
milk	mjölk (-en)
money	pengar
money back guarantee	bytesrätt, returrätt (-en -er)
more	mer
morning	morgon (-en morgnar)
most often	oftast
move	flytt/a (-ar -ade -at)
mulled wine	glögg (-en)
must	måste
name	namn (-et -0)

national bank	riksbank (-en -er)
naturally, of course	naturligtvis
near, close	nära
need	behöv/a (-er -de -t)
nervous	nervös
never	aldrig
next	nästa
nice	trevlig
night	natt (-en nätter)
no	nej
non-smoker	icke-rökare (-n -0)
not at all	inte alls
note down	anteckn/a (-ar -ade -at)
nowadays	nuförtiden
nursery	dagis (-et -0)
offer	erbjud/a (-er erbjöd erbjudit)
one each	var sin
only	bara
organize	ordn/a (-ar -ade -at)
others	andra
outdated	inaktuell
outside	ute, utomhus
oven	ugn (-en -ar)
oven, stove, fireplace	spis (-en -ar)
over, above	över
park	parker/a (-ar -ade -at)
partly	delvis
party	fest (-en -er)
passport	pass(-et -0)
pay	betal/a (-ar -ade -at)
pea soup	ärtsopp/a (-an -or)
peace	fred (-en)
pedestrian	fotgängare (-n -0)
pedestrian crossing	övergångsställ/e (-et -en)
petrol	bensin (-en)
physical education, gymnastics	gymnastik (-en)
physics	fysik (-en)
place	plats (-en -er)
plan	plan (-en -er), planer/a (-ar -ade -at)
pleasant	skönt
please	varsågod
potato	potatis (-en -ar)
practice	öv/a (-ar -ade -at), övning (-en -ar)
pray, beg	be (-r bad bett)
precisely, exactly	precis
price	pris (-et -er)
probably	troligen
promise	lov/a (-ar -ade -at)
provide, get	skaff/a (-ar -ade -at)
question	fråg/a (-an -or)
quite simply	helt enkelt

quite, exactly	alldeles
rain	regn (-et -0)
raspberry	hallon (-et -0)
really, certainly	verkligen
receipt	kvitto (-t -n)
remember	minnas (minns mindes)
rent	hyr/a (-0 -de -t)
ride	rid/a (-er red ridit)
right	höger
right, correct	riktigt
room	rum (-met -0)
roundabout	rondell (-en -er)
safe, secure	säker
saint	helgon (-et -0)
salmon	lax (-en -ar)
same	samma
satisfied	nöjd
sauna	bastu (-n -r)
season	årstid (-en -er)
seatbelt	säkerhetsbält/e (-et -en)
see	se (såg sett)
seem	verk/a (-ar -ade -at)
self-evident, obvious	självklart
serve	server/a (-ar -ade -at)
shall, will	ska (skulle)
ship	skepp (-et -0)
shoe	sko (-n -r)
shop	affär (-en -er)
show	vis/a (-ar -ade -at)
shower	dusch (-en -ar)
shrimp	räk/a (-an -or)
sign	skylt (-en -ar), teck/en (-net -0)
simplify	förenkl/a (-ar -ade -at)
sing	sjung/a (-er sjöng sjungit)
sit	sitt/a (-er satt suttit)
size	storlek (-en -ar)
ski	skid/a (-an -or)
skin	skinn (-et -0)
sleep	sov/a (-er sov sovit)
sleeper	sovvagn (-en -ar)
slip, sneak	smyg/a (-er smög smugit)
slown down	sakt/a (-ar -ade -at) ner
smoking ban	rökförbud (-et -0)
snow	snö (-n)
so	så
soon	snart, strax
sorry, (I am sorry)	förlåt
soup	sopp/a (-an -or)
spoon	sked (-en -ar)
spring	vår (-en -ar)
starter	förrätt (-en -er)
stay	vistelse (-n -r)

still	fortfarande
stop	stann/a (-ar -ade -at)
straight across	tvärs över
straight ahead	rakt fram
strawberry	jordgubb/e (-en -ar)
street	gat/a (-an -or)
such	sådan
suggestion	förslag (-et -0)
suitcase	väsk/a (-an -or)
summer	sommar (-en somrar)
super!	jättebra
sweater	tröj/a (-an -or)
table	bord (-et -0)
take	ta (-r tog tagit)
take out	plock/a (-ar -ade -at) fram
take turns	tur/as (-0 -ades -ats) om
task	uppgift (-en -er)
taste	smak (-en -er)
tasty	smaklig
teaspoon	tesked (-en -ar)
tennis court	tennisban/a (-an -or)
thanks	tack
then	då
then, later	sedan
think of	tänk/a (-er -te -t) på
think; like	tyck/a (-er -te -t) om
thrilling	spännande
ticket	biljett (-en -er)
tie a knot	knyt/a (-er knöt knutit)
time	tid (-en -er)
timetable	schem/a (-at -an), tidtabell (-en -er)
to, until	till, tills
town, city	stad (-en städer)
traditional basic food	husmanskost (-en)
train	tåg (-et -0)
travel	res/a (-er -te -t)
tray	brick/a (-n -or)
tree	träd (-et -0)
trousers	byx/a (- n -or)
try, test	prov/a, pröv/a (-ar -ade -at)
tulip	tulpan (-en -er)
tumble dryer	torktumlare (-n -0)
turn into	sväng/a (-er -de -t) in
turn, luck	tur (-en)
unfortunately	dessvärre, tyvärr
until then	till dess
unusual	ovanlig
up to date, topical	aktuell
use	använd/a (-er -e använt)
usually do	bruk/a (-ar -ade -at)
variety, variation	omväxling (-en)

very, much	mycket
view	utsikt (-en -er)
visit	påhälsning (-en -ar), besök (-et -0)
wait	vänt/a (-ar -ade -at)
walk, stroll	promener/a (-ar -ade -at)
walk, wander	vandr/a (-ar -ade -at)
war	krig (-et -0)
wash up	disk/a (-ar -ade -at)
watercolour	akvarellmålning (-en -ar)
way home	hemväg (-en -ar)
way, road	väg (-en -ar)
wealth	förmögenhet (-en -er)
weather	väd/er (-ret -0)
wedding	bröllop (-et -0)
week	veck/a (-an -or)
weekday, every day	vardag (-en -ar)
welcome	välkommen
well liked	omtyckt
wet	blöt, våt
while, because	eftersom
whipped cream	vispgrädde (-n)
Whitsun evening	pingstafton (-en -aftnar)
window	fönst/er (-ret -0)
winter	vint/er (-ern -rar)
with	med
woman	fruntim/mer (-ret -0), kvinn/a (-an -or)
work	arbet/a (-ar -ade -at), jobb/a (-ar -ade -at)
world	värld (-en -ar)
write	skriv/a (-er skrev skrivit)
year	år (-et -0)
yes, yes of course	ja, javisst

Image credits

Pages: 2, 22 (Hotell Sekelgården, Ystad), 32, 34, 46, 66 (Fridolfs Konditori, Ystad), 68, 78, 98 and 108: Ivo Holmqvist

Page 56: Ingwor Holmqvist

Page 88: Massimo Federici

Page 9: G Tipene/Shutterstock.com

Page 18: Ramona Heim/Shutterstock.com

Voice credits

Recorded at Alchemy Studios, London

Cast: Lisa Gustafsson, Kristina Bill, Gunnar Petterson, Matt Akesson, Sarah Sherborne